Women in the Arts

Virginia Woolf

He who neglects the arts when he is young
has lost the past and is dead to the future.

—Sophocles, *Fragments*

Virginia Woolf

Cliff Mills

Introduction by
Congresswoman Betty McCollum
Minnesota, Fourth District
Member, National Council on the Arts

CHELSEA HOUSE
PUBLISHERS
A Haights Cross Communications Company
Philadelphia

CHELSEA HOUSE PUBLISHERS
VP, New Product Development Sally Cheney
Director of Production Kim Shinners
Creative Manager Takeshi Takahashi
Manufacturing Manager Diann Grasse

Staff for VIRGINIA WOOLF
Editor Patrick M. N. Stone
Production Editor Megan Emery
Assistant Photo Editor Noelle Nardone
Series & Cover Designer Terry Mallon
Layout 21st Century Publishing and Communications, Inc.

A Haights Cross Communications ✦ Company

www.chelseahouse.com

First Printing

1 3 5 7 9 8 6 4 2

Library of Congress Cataloging-in-Publication Data

Mills, Clifford, 1947–
    Virginia Woolf/by Clifford Mills.
        p. cm. — (Women in the arts)
Summary: Discusses the life and work of the twentieth century English
author, Virginia Woolf. Includes bibliographical references and index.
    ISBN 0-7910-7459-5 (Hardcover)   0-7910-7953-8 PB
    1. Woolf, Virginia, 1882–1941 — Juvenile literature. 2. Novelists,
English — 20th century — Biography — Juvenile literature. 3. Women
and literature — England — History — 20th century — Juvenile literature.
[1. Woolf, Virginia, 1882–1941. 2. Authors, English. 3. Women —
Biography.] I. Title. II. Women in the arts (Philadelphia, Pa.) III. Title.
PR6045.O72Z8169 2003
823'.912 — dc21

                                                          2003009505

Table of Contents

Introduction

Congresswoman Betty McCollum
Minnesota, Fourth District
Member, National Council on the Arts

I am honored to introduce WOMEN IN THE ARTS, a continuing series of books about courageous, talented women whose work has changed the way we think about art and society. The women highlighted in this series were persistent, successful, and at times controversial. They were unafraid to ask questions or challenge social norms while pursuing their work. They overcame barriers that included discrimination, prejudice, and poverty. The energy, creativity, and perseverance of these strong women changed our world forever.

Art plays a critical role in all our lives, in every culture, and especially in the education of young people. Art can be serious, beautiful, functional, provocative, spiritual, informative, and illuminating. For all of the women in this series, their respective forms of artistic expression were a creative exploration and their professional calling. Their lives and their work transformed the world's perception of a woman's role in society.

In reading this series, I was struck by common themes evident in these women's lives that can provide valuable lessons for today's young women.

One volume tells the story of Coco Chanel, the first fashion designer to create clothing for women that was both attractive and utile. Chanel was one of the first women to run a large, successful business in the fashion industry. Today, it is hard to imagine the controversy Chanel stirred up simply by making women's clothing beautiful, comfortable, and practical. Chanel understood that women wanted a sense of style and professionalism in their fashion, as men had in theirs.

Chanel's extraordinary success demonstrates that we should not be afraid to be controversial. Even today, women of all ages worry far too much about stepping on toes or questioning authority. To make change, in our own lives or in our community, we need to stand up and speak out for our beliefs. The women of this series often defied convention and ruffled some feathers, but they never stopped. Nina Simone sang beautifully, but she also spoke out against the injustice of racism, regardless of how it affected her career.

It is equally important for us women to ask ourselves, "What do I want from my life?" We all struggle to answer this deceptively simple question. It takes courage to answer it honestly, but it takes far more courage to answer the question and then *act* on that answer. For example, Agnes de Mille realized she had "nothing to lose by being direct." She stuck to her vision for *Rodeo,* insisted on the set and composer she envisioned, and eventually produced her ballet—the way she wanted to. She believed in her vision, and the result was a great success. Dorothea Lange, having decided she wanted to become a photographer, asked for photography jobs, even though she had no experience and it was a profession that few women pursued.

In our society, we expect that all people should be treated with respect and dignity, but this has not always been true. Nina Simone faced discrimination and overcame social norms that promoted racial injustice. She confronted prejudice and disrespect directly, sometimes refusing to perform when an audience was unruly or rude. One evening, when she was only eleven years old, she even delayed her performance until her own parents were allowed to sit in the front row—seats that they had been asked to vacate for white people. Her demand for respect took courage.

Women's equality not only benefits women, but also brings a unique perspective to the world. For example, the brilliance of Dorothea Lange's photography was in large part due to her empathy for her subjects. She knew that to tell their story, she needed to earn their trust and to truly understand their lives.

Each of these women used her art to promote social justice. Coco Chanel used her designs to make women's lives easier and more comfortable, while Nina Simone was as committed to civil rights as she was to her music. Dorothea Lange's photographs convinced Washington of the need to establish sanitary camps for migrant families, and Virginia Woolf's writing pushed the question of equal rights for women.

Because the women in these books, and so many others like them, took risks and challenged society, women today have more opportunity than ever before. We have access to equal education, and we are making great strides in the workplace and in government.

As only the second woman from Minnesota ever elected to serve in Congress, I know how important it is to have strong female role models. My grandmothers were born in a time when women did not have the right to vote, but their granddaughter is now a Member of Congress. Their strength, wisdom, and courage inspire me. Other great women, such as Congresswoman Barbara Jordan and Congresswoman Shirley Chisholm, also inspired me with their leadership and determination to overcome gender and racial discrimination to serve in Congress with distinction.

Dorothea Lange once said, "I have learned from everything, and I'm constantly learning." I know that I too am constantly learning. I hope the women in this series will inspire you to learn and to lead with courage and determination. Art, as a profession or a hobby, can be either an expression or an agent of change. We need to continue to encourage women to add their voices to our society through art.

The women profiled in this series broke barriers, followed their hearts, refused to be intimidated, and changed our world. Their lives and successes should be a lesson to women everywhere. In addition, and importantly, they created lasting and meaningful art. I hope that you will enjoy this series as much as I have.

Fame Captures Virginia Woolf

Literature is strewn with the wreckage of men who have minded beyond reason the opinions of others.

—Virginia Woolf, *A Room of One's Own* (1929)

TIME FOR FAME

The year 1937 was among "the worst of times"—a year of international state-sponsored terrorism and economic uncertainty. Adolf Hitler and Benito Mussolini were increasing the scale of their violence in Europe, and the world had yet to escape from the Great Depression. The American magazine *Time* gave its readers a break from this grim reality when it featured a "new and exciting" writer on the cover of its issue for April 12, 1937. The writer was a woman with a strong profile and striking face. The caption read: "Virginia Woolf: 'It is fatal to be man or woman pure and simple.'"

TIME

The Weekly Newsmagazine

Man Ray

VIRGINIA WOOLF

Volume XXIX

"It is fatal to be a man or woman pure and simple."
(See BOOKS)

Number 15

International acclaim. Woolf's appearance on the cover of *Time* in early 1937 brought her name far beyond her homeland of Great Britain and into the international arena. Although she was perpetually shy and critical of her work, exposure like this increased her tremendous success as an author and sparked interest for her writing in the hearts of readers worldwide. At this point, in 1937, Woolf had already written *To the Lighthouse*, *Orlando*, *A Room of One's Own*, *Mrs. Dalloway*, *The Waves*, and other works, and it was understood that she would have a profound impact on the literature of the time.

Woolf was well-known to many in her homeland of Great Britain, but her appearance on the cover of *Time* caused her popularity to spread around the world. The writer of the cover article even predicted that Woolf's fame would place her among the great figures of literature, calling her "not just a highbrow writer but perhaps a great one." Her star status faded somewhat over the next thirty years, only to burn more brightly in the 1970s and later. Among critics, she is considered one of the most influential writers of modern fiction, a woman who experimented with the English language and literary conventions and left both changed forever.

Despite her popularity, Woolf tended to avoid the public spotlight and was protective of her privacy and writing time. When asked about the parade of people coming to visit and interview her, she wrote, "I like when people come, but I love when they go." (Nicolson, 136) She was always shy, and she declined many honors that required public speaking. Still, she recognized the benefits of advertising and must have been relieved when the *Time* cover helped her newest book, *The Years*, to become a best-seller. Critical of her own work, Woolf thought *The Years* was "a long weary dreary book" and was afraid it would not sell well. (Nicolson, 146) She need not have worried; the novel's candid attitudes toward sex, war, the trials of youth, and the conflicts between rich and poor took the literary world by storm.

AN EXTRAORDINARY MIND AT WORK

Woolf recorded the details of her life, including her desires, thrills, dreams, annoyances, hatreds, and fears in journals and personal correspondence. She kept a diary from the age of fifteen and wrote as many as six letters a day. In addition to finding personal compositions soothing, she used these informal writings to practice her craft, experimenting with words, images, and metaphors. Woolf never intended for the public to read these intimate writings (her husband, Leonard, published her diaries and letters posthumously against her wishes); however, these writings have provided Woolf scholars with a rare glimpse of her extraordinary mind at work.

Beyond her letters and diaries, Virginia Woolf played with and often broke writing conventions. She wrote novels

WOOLF ON THE INVISIBLE WOMAN

From *A Room of One's Own*:

[T]he majority of women are neither harlots nor courtesans; nor do they sit clasping pug dogs to dusty velvet all through the summer afternoon. But what do they do then? and there came to my mind's eye one of those long streets somewhere south of the river whose infinite rows are innumerably populated. With the eye of the imagination I saw a very ancient lady crossing the street on the arm of a middle-aged woman, her daughter, perhaps. . . . The elder is close on eighty; but if one asked her what her life has meant to her, she would say that she remembered the streets lit for the battle of Balaclava, or had heard the guns fire in Hyde Park for the birth of King Edward the Seventh. And if one asked her, longing to pin down the moment with date and season, but what were you doing on the fifth of April 1868, or the second of November 1875, she would look vague and say that she could remember nothing. For all the dinners are cooked; the plates and cups washed; the children sent to school and gone out into the world. Nothing remains of it all. All has vanished. No biography or history has a word to say about it. And the novels, without meaning to, inevitably lie.

All these infinitely obscure lives remain to be recorded. . . .

that contained plays and poems, stories that read like essays, and biographies that read like fiction. She started her career as a journalist, writing about subjects such as architecture, aviation, travel, and emerging technologies. Later, she composed essays, biographies, traditional fiction, and experimental novels. Due to the breadth and complexity of her writings, some critics have considered her more a poet than a novelist. Her texts, never pure and simple, have enabled generations of readers to invoke her ideas in discussions about feminism, multiculturalism, "highbrow" versus "lowbrow" culture and entertainment, political correctness, civil rights, and gay and lesbian rights. Her ideas challenged people to treasure their private lives, to respect their differences, to fight repression of all kinds, and to transform traumatic experiences into learning opportunities.

A LIFE OF CONTRADICTIONS

Woolf's life and lifestyle were as shockingly progressive as her writing. Her life was filled with tensions and contractions. She had bursts of intense creativity and crippling bouts of mental illness. She loved several men and women deeply, including her husband Leonard Woolf and Vita Sackville-West, an aristocratic celebrity authoress. Woolf experienced personal triumphs, such as the success her writing and publishing brought her, and she knew personal tragedies, including the deaths of her parents, her brother, and her half-brother by the time she was twenty-two. She never received a college education or attended high school, but she was extremely well educated. She had a gift for friendship and loved to listen to people; however, people whose wit and intelligence could not keep up with those of her and her friends were often the subject of her sharp tongue and pen. When her friend Lytton Strachey was criticized by an acquaintance, she wrote, "Lytton has more love in his little finger than that castrated cat in the whole of his mangy, stringy, partless, gutless, tailess body." (Nicolson, 137–138) Even at her most depressed, she never neglected her friends or her family.

Her lifestyle also defied convention. After the deaths of her parents, Woolf and her siblings moved to Bloomsbury, a questionable neighborhood for upper-class children. There, she and her sister Vanessa engaged in discussions with their brother's Cambridge friends as equals. The Bloomsbury Group, as they were later known, discussed academic, artistic, political, and even sexual subjects—no topic was sacred. Each member exaggerated the faults of the others for sport; indeed, some said the difference between the Bloomsbury gatherings and Cambridge was that at Cambridge nothing funny was ever said unless it was also philosophical, and at Bloomsbury nothing philosophical was ever said that wasn't also funny. The group generally accepted homosexuality, and many practiced it; they also considered extramarital affairs normal. Their frank recognition of these "deviancies" contrasted sharply with the prudish Victorian values set by the previous generation and gained the group the notoriety it became famous for. Biographer Hermione Lee quotes Woolf's recollection: "Sex permeated our conversation. . . . We discussed copulation with the same excitement and openness that we had discussed the nature of good. . . . [Before the war] when all intellectual questions had been debated so freely, sex was ignored. Now a flood of light poured in upon that department too. We had known every-thing but we had never talked. Now we talked of nothing else. . . ." (Lee, 196–196)

The *Time* cover that fueled her popularity in 1937 helped to fulfill the prediction that Woolf would one day be heralded as a leading literary figure. Since the 1930s, her image has been used to inspire change and has become synonymous with feminism, creative experimentalism, disestablishment, and sexual tolerance. Her essays and fiction

Lytton Strachey. Giles Lytton Strachey (1880–1932),
widely considered a successor to Oscar Wilde's wit, was
one of Woolf's greatest friends. He was also a vital and
somewhat scandalous member of the Bloomsbury Group,
and his *Eminent Victorians* (1918) is counted among the
key antiestablishment Bloomsbury works. Woolf supported
him without question, even sharply lambasting his critics.
His death in 1932 seriously affected her mental and physical
health. (Strachey's longtime admirer Dora Carrington, a
peripheral member of the Bloomsbury Group, took her own
life soon afterward.)

have been incorporated into the academic canon for English literature and have withstood the test of time, despite critics' attempts to categorize her writing. This ability of her works to defy interpretation only strengthens her position among the literary elite.

2

A Childhood Bright and Shattered

1882–1905

The interest in life does not lie in what people do, nor even in their relations to each other, but largely in the power to communicate with a third party, antagonistic, enigmatic, yet perhaps persuadable, which one may call life in general.

—Virginia Woolf, "On Not Knowing Greek" (1925)

Young women[,] . . . you are, in my opinion, disgracefully ignorant. You have never made a discovery of any sort of importance. You have never shaken an empire or led an army into battle. The plays by Shakespeare are not by you, and you have never introduced a barbarous race to the blessings of civilization. What is your excuse?

—Virginia Woolf, *A Room of One's Own* (1929)

THE STEPHENS

Virginia Woolf was born Adeline Virginia Stephen on January 25, 1882, in London, at 22 Hyde Park Gate, the third child of aristocratic and intellectual parents. Her father was Leslie Stephen, a well-known journalist, editor, philosopher, and literary figure in England. He had come to London from his hometown of Cambridge in 1859 with no money and no job prospects. Finding work as a journalist, Leslie traveled to America to meet and interview Abraham Lincoln, James Russell Lowell, and Oliver Wendell Holmes. He embraced many controversial views. For example, he was sympathetic to the United States and Lincoln in the American Civil War. Like his father and grandfather, Leslie hated slavery and advocated its abolition. Still, he upheld the puritanical values of the Victorian era. The year Woolf was born he became the editor for *The Dictionary of National Biography*. As editor, he befriended the great writers of the day, including Matthew Arnold, Thomas Carlyle, George Eliot, Thomas Hardy, and Henry James.

Woolf's mother was Julia (Jackson) Stephen, a beautiful model who had posed for several famous painters and photographers. Unlike her husband, Julia radiated confidence and self-assurance. She encouraged wit in her children and dominated Leslie with her submissiveness. Although initially reluctant to wed the middle-aged, conservative Leslie, Julia had fallen in love after a slow courtship. Leslie and Julia Stephen were married on March 26, 1878.

The Stephens lived in a large, wealthy section of London, and their house was often bustling with activity. Aside from relatives, scholars, artists, and friends who visited continually, both Julia and Leslie had been married and widowed before their first meeting. They both had children from previous marriages. Leslie had a daughter named Laura Stephen from his marriage to Harriet Marian Thackeray, who had died in childbirth; Julia had sons George and Gerald and daughter Stella, all of whom bore the surname of their father Herbert Duckworth. After their wedding, Julia and Leslie had their own four children in rapid succession: Vanessa (1879),

Virginia Stephen with her father, c. 1900. Woolf acquired many of her "social activist" traits from her father, an outspoken and prolific journalist and editor who enjoyed a very wide acquaintance in literary circles. The two got along well and shared many ideas about life and politics. Woolf's father was her main tutor and guide in her literary education, and, as a scholar himself, he encouraged her love of reading.

Julian Thoby (1880, called Thoby), Virginia (1882), and Adrian (1883).

The children adored their parents. In 1907, Woolf wrote, "Beautiful often, even to our eyes, were their gestures, their glances of pure and unutterable delight in each other." (Nicolson, 4) The Stephens were supportive of each other and of their children. Altogether, they were a happy, talented family whose affections for one another dispelled any tensions.

As a child, Woolf worried her parents. She did not talk until she was almost four years old, and they feared she might have developmental problems. When she did learn to speak, she learned the private language created by the Stephen children, and her parents were relieved to see her share private jokes with her siblings. Around this time, Vanessa became protective of her younger siblings, and the four Stephen children became very close. They were sensitive to one another's needs and involved with one another's interests, and they remained much closer than the Duckworth children were. This friendship among the Stephen children remained all their lives. In particular, Woolf admired Vanessa, relishing her older sister's calm honesty and quiet practicality that was so similar to their mother's.

WOOLF'S EDUCATION

When the Stephen children reached school age, Julia and Leslie decided to educate the children at home, an unusual decision given their lower-upper-class status and the time period. Julia taught them Latin, history, and French, while Leslie taught math. Leslie was an impatient teacher and became angry whenever the children had trouble grasping mathematical concepts. As a result, only Thoby learned math; Woolf's math expertise was limited to counting on her fingers.

Despite unpleasant math lessons, Leslie endeared himself to Woolf by allowing her full access to his extensive library. This was a rare freedom for a young girl, and Woolf took full advantage of it. Initially, Leslie guided her choices, but soon he was unable to keep up with her appetite for learning. He found that she was "devouring books almost faster than I like." Still, Leslie encouraged her reading and writing and frequently discussed literature with her. His letters to Julia revealed his hope that Woolf might one day become his literary and intellectual heir, stating, "Yesterday I discussed George II with 'Ginia. She takes in a great deal and will really be an author in time; though I cannot make up my mind in what line. History will be a good thing for her to take up as I can give her some hints." At the time of these comments, Woolf was eleven. When her interests leaned toward the classics, Leslie paid for lessons in Latin and Greek, so that she could read Homer and Sophocles. Perhaps, through reading, Woolf secured her father's favor and gained the attention she craved. (Leaska, 75)

When the Stephen boys were sent away to school, Vanessa and Woolf continued their home education with tutors to instruct them in music, riding, and dance. Woolf was never accomplished at music and hated both dance and piano lessons. Instead, she honed her talents for mockery and observation through her letters to family and friends. She resented her informal education and wished for the same education as her brothers. "Think how I was brought up!" she later wrote to Vita Sackville-West. "No school; mooning about alone among my father's books; never any chance to pick up all that goes on in schools—throwing balls; ragging; slang; vulgarities; scenes; jealousies!" (Nicolson, 9) Woolf also resented what she deemed her inadequate schooling, and as an adult, she became an outspoken advocate for equality in education.

To channel her budding literary talents, Woolf initiated ways to express herself. She and Thoby started a family news-paper, *The Hyde Park News*, that they distributed to family and friends. Although Woolf was only nine when the newspaper began, most of the articles were attributed to her, as Thoby was already away at school. She reported on events at home and on vacation, and scholars have linked material in her articles to some of her later masterpieces. For example, in an article dated September 12, 1892, Woolf reports,

On Saturday morning Master Hilary Hunt and Master Basil Smith came up to Talland House and asked Master Thoby and Miss Virginia Stephen to accompany them to the light-house as Freeman the boatman said that there was a perfect wind and tide for going there. Master Adrian Stephen was much disappointed at not being allowed to go. (Lehmann, 12)

Julia Stephen. Woolf's mother, Julia (Jackson) Stephen, was a talented, outgoing woman, strong in her own abilities. She passed this determination and self-assurance along to her daughter, preparing her to be one of the boldest writers of her time. Woolf never thought of their relationship as a close one, though; she wrote long after her mother's death that the demands of the family had always sapped Julia's energies. "Mother figures" are prominent in much of Woolf's work.

This incident may have been a reference for her later novel *To the Lighthouse*. When her mother read the paper and thought it clever, Woolf was ecstatic. Due to tragic family events, the paper ended its run in 1895.

PARADISE LOST

The children's favorite annual event was the family trip to the ocean at St. Ives. They stayed in Talland House, which Leslie had purchased the year Woolf was born. The house overlooked the bay and a lighthouse and provided the perfect setting for adolescent amusements. Woolf loved to wade in the tidal pools with their sea anemones and blue lobsters. The children also played on the shore, fished, and boated. They enjoyed cricket, at which Woolf was very talented, and often played late into the summer evenings. The cricket field also provided a multitude of bugs that the children liked to collect. Trips to the nearby lighthouse were especially exciting, providing Woolf with rich images for her writing. Summers at St. Ives gave her a sense of true happiness; this was the Eden of her youth, a place of "pure delight." (Nicolson, 8)

This paradise was lost forever when Julia suddenly died from rheumatic fever on May 15, 1895. Woolf was thirteen. She later wrote, "Her death was the greatest disaster that could happen." (Lehmann, 13) The Stephen family fractured after Julia's death. Leslie had always worried about his health, his reputation, and his money, and Julia had always helped to soothe his worries and provide support. With her gone, Leslie isolated himself, sitting at meals barely hearing, crying in front of his children, and proclaiming his desire to die. He refused to return to St. Ives and Talland House, and his children were alienated from the source of their happy childhood memories.

To make matters worse, Julia's sons George and Gerald (Woolf's half-brothers) took advantage of the chaos and lack of supervision following Julia's death to engage in questionable activities with Vanessa and Woolf. A few incidents even took

WOOLF AND HER MOTHER

Many critics have noted that in Woolf's fiction the mother figure is a source of happiness, order, and continuity. Clarissa Dalloway in *Mrs. Dalloway* and Lily Briscoe in *To the Lighthouse* struggle to keep their families together, with the threat of disintegration always present. It is possible that losing her mother played a role in Woolf's creation of these themes. In *Moments of Being*, Woolf describes her own mother as crucial and central but, because of that importance, distant and inaccessible:

> I suspect the word 'central' gets closest to the general feeling I had of living so completely in her atmosphere that one never got far enough away from her to see her as a person. . . . She was the whole thing; [the house in Cornwall] was full of her; Hyde Park Gate [in London] was full of her. I see now, though the sentence is hasty, feeble and inexpressive, why it was that it was impossible for her to leave a very private and particular impression upon a child. She was keeping what I call in my shorthand the panoply of life—that which we all lived in common—in being. . . . The later view, the understanding that I now have of her position must have its say; and it shows me that a woman of forty with seven children, some of them needing grown-up attention, and four still in the nursery; and an eighth, Laura, an idiot, yet living with us; and a husband fifteen years her elder, difficult, exacting, dependent on her; I see now that a woman who had to keep all this in being and under control must have been a general presence rather than a particular person to a child of seven or eight. Can I remember ever being alone with her for more than a few minutes? Someone was always interrupting. ("A Sketch of the Past," 83)

place well before Julia died. Woolf recalled one incident at St. Ives when she was six years old in which Gerald fondled her private parts, but George was the main offender. He would "enter [Woolf's] bedroom, fling himself onto her bed, and take her in his arms . . . [in] violent gusts of passion." (Nicolson, 11) In her letters, Woolf implied that George had an incestuous relationship with both her and Vanessa, but critics disagree about the extent of his sexual indiscretions. Woolf herself seems to have regarded George affectionately as a friend in later years and addressed her letters to him "My dear old Bar" and "My Dearest George," and Vanessa happily accompanied him to Paris and Rome in 1898 and 1900. (Nicolson, 12) Still, George's inappropriate behavior clearly influenced and stunted Woolf's sexuality. Many of her fictional characters also experienced childhood traumas. In *The Waves*, she writes, "what awful lives children live. . . . And they can't tell anybody." With no one to confide in, Woolf repressed her feelings, and fears of invasion haunted her for the rest of her life.

NEW DEPTHS

The twin traumas of her mother's death and her half-brothers' sexual abuse led to Woolf's first mental breakdown. In her diary, she wrote that she felt her face pulse and heard terrible voices. She became extremely self-critical and often compared herself unfavorably to Vanessa. She stopped writing entirely and, instead, read voraciously. She collapsed mentally and physically. Various causes of her mental instability have been identified; what is certain is that Woolf continued to suffer from periodic episodes of mental illness for the rest of her life.

Slowly the symptoms of her first breakdown receded and, with Vanessa's help, Woolf resumed her diminished life. Her father offered little assistance in her recovery. He became more withdrawn as his financial concerns overwhelmed him. He continued to enjoy the company of his friends, but he frequently vented his frustrations on his children. For a time, he directed most of his anger toward Stella Duckworth (Julia's eldest daughter), who filled Julia's role as head of the household. When Stella married and soon after died, Vanessa inherited the household accounts and became the object of his temper. To escape him, Woolf immersed herself further in Leslie's books.

She also developed a new distraction. She began to participate in the social activities befitting of a young woman. She entertained guests at 4:30 P.M. tea in the front room of the house, inviting family, friends, relatives, and neighbors. Woolf realized that these activities enabled her to learn the art of conversation, small talk, and flattery, skills undeveloped by her home education. She learned to placate people whom Leslie offended, and she found to her amazement that she enjoyed social gatherings. Dances, however, she disliked, as she had a terrible habit of blushing whenever she was spoken to. She wrote, "[I] can't shine in society. I don't know how it's done. We ain't popular. We sit in corners and look like mutes who are longing for a funeral." (Nicolson, 13) Attending a dinner at a countess's house, though, she spoke with such confidence that her hostess was surprised to find her so bold in mixed company. Woolf found a certain gallantry in socially successful people, and she was determined to succeed in society. By watching others, she cultivated her social sophistication and began to understand group dynamics, an understanding that she explored in many of her novels.

Sir Leslie Stephen was diagnosed with abdominal cancer in 1902; two years later, on February 22, 1904, he died. Woolf was heartbroken. She wrote to her friend Janet Case:

> Father died very peacefully, as we sat by him. I know it was what he wanted most. All these years we have hardly been apart and I want him every moment of the day. But we still have each other—Nessa and Thoby and Adrian and I, and when we are together, he and Mother do not seem far off. (Nicolson, 14)

Sir Leslie Stephen. Although an impatient math teacher, Woolf's father was eager to encourage her literary appetite. He provided her with an extensive library, and eventually he even found it difficult to keep up with her voracious reading. He enjoyed talking about authors and literary subjects with his daughter, hoping that she would follow in his footsteps as a writer. His death in 1904 inspired the Stephen children's trip to Wales, where Virginia made the decision to become a writer, and was a major factor in her second major episode of mental illness.

As with their mother's death, the Stephen children grew even closer after Leslie died, seeking solace and support from each other.

To mourn in peace, the Stephen children left London and traveled to Manorbier in southern Wales soon after Leslie's cremation. There, Woolf pondered her future and decided that she should become a writer. She wrote, "That vision came to me more clearly at Manorbier aged 21 [22], walking the down on the edge of the sea." (Leaska, 95) She had considered writing a book for several years, but it was not until her father's death that she became motivated to do so.

After Manorbier, the Stephen children traveled to Italy and France to further distract themselves and recover from their father's death. Woolf was delighted by the Italian countryside, but she disliked the people. In Paris, they met Clive Bell, a friend of Thoby's from Cambridge. Bell took the Stephens to visit Auguste Rodin's studio, and Woolf enjoyed his company. Their friendship might have developed quickly had Woolf not experienced a second mental breakdown on her return from Paris. Like her first episode, the second one began with headaches and fits of confusion. It then progressed to over-whelming guilt over her father's death. Her agitation grew, and her family moved her back to the country to calm her. The move did not help. She resisted her three nurses, whom she considered evil, and attempted suicide by jumping from an open window. Luckily, the window was too close to the ground for a fatal effect, and she was not seriously injured. The madness passed slowly with the help of her close friend Violet Dickinson, with whom Virginia had very likely fallen in love.

Sent to live with relatives to recuperate from her illness, Woolf renewed her interest in writing. In November of 1904, she visited Haworth Parsonage, the home of the Brontë sisters, and submitted an account of her visit to the newspaper, *The Guardian.* This piece, her first to be accepted for publication, appeared on December 21 of the same year. Woolf was disturbed to note that the editor had made minor cuts and changes to her work; in 1905, she complained to Violet that *The Guardian*'s editor "sticks her broad thumb into the middle of my delicate sentences and improves the moral tone." (Leaska, 117) Nevertheless, even in this early work, Woolf shows a clear talent for evoking the human drama within the mundane details of everyday life:

> I do not know whether pilgrimages to the shrines of famous men ought not to be condemned as sentimental journeys. It is better to read Carlyle in your own study chair than to visit the sound-proof room and pore over the manuscripts at Chelsea. . . . The curiosity is only legitimate when the house of a great writer or the country in which it is set adds something to our understanding of his books. This justification you have for a pilgrimage to the home and country of Charlotte Bronte and her sisters.
>
> . . . The house . . . is precisely the same as it was in Charlotte's day, save that one new wing has been added. It is easy to shut the eye to this, and then you have the square, boxlike parsonage, built of the ugly yellow-brown stone which they quarry from the moors behind, precisely as it was when Charlotte lived and died there. Inside, of course, the changes are many, though not such as to obscure the original shape of the rooms. There is nothing remarkable in a mid-Victorian parsonage, though tenanted by genius, and the only room which awakens curiosity is the kitchen, now used as an anteroom, in which the girls tramped as they conceived their work. One other spot has a certain grim interest—the oblong recess beside the staircase into which Emily drove her bulldog during the famous fight, and pinned him while she pommelled him. It is otherwise a little sparse parsonage, much like others of its kind.

And, regardless of her frustrations with the editorial process, she was published and earning money. Soon, she was writing reviews for *The Times Literary Supplement* and longer articles for the monthly magazine *Cornhill.*

Just like her father, Woolf had become a professional writer. She had survived the deaths of her parents, abuse by her brothers, and two mental breakdowns. Little did she know, she was poised to begin a life of achievement and secure her place in history.

The Birth of the Bloomsbury Group

1905–1910

. . . [I]t is fatal for anyone who writes to think of their sex. It is fatal to be a man or woman pure and simple; one must be woman-manly or man-womanly.

> —Virginia Woolf, *A Room of One's Own* (1929)

Let a man get up and say, "Behold, this is the truth," and instantly I perceive a sandy cat filching a piece of fish in the background. Look, you have forgotten the cat, I say.

> —Virginia Woolf, *The Waves* (1931)

A FRESH START

During Woolf's second breakdown and recovery, the Stephen children finalized their plans to leave 22 Hyde Park Gate and escape the Duckworths' supervision. Shocking their family and friends, they moved away from Kensington and relocated to a large house at 46 Gordon Square in Bloomsbury. The new

The outspoken Virginia Woolf. **Although appearing mild and quiet in photos, Woolf was outspoken on a range of social issues. Her growing affinity for social interaction and discussion during her early years with the Bloomsbury Group fueled the appetite to fight for social justice that is so evident in all her works. It was this attitude that permitted Woolf to speak on previously unaddressed social issues such as homosexuality and women's rights; her extended essay *A Room of One's Own* (1929) is among the first "feminist" essays, an essay that seriously considers the lack of female writers in history.**

neighborhood consisted of a lower class of people and was known for its acceptance of bohemian lifestyles. In Bloomsbury, they could live free from familial expectations; they dressed as they wanted, ate when they wished, and left unimportant acquaintances behind. In short, they reinvented themselves.

At Vanessa's suggestion, Thoby began to invite friends from Cambridge to the house for dinners and parties. Quickly, 46 Gordon Square became an intellectual center for "twentysomethings" wanting to discuss subjects such as art, literature, science, and politics. The meetings occurred on Thursday and Friday nights, and the people who formed the core of the gatherings came to include the most influential young scholars and artists of the day: Lytton Strachey, a brilliant writer who changed the literary form of biography and whose harsh criticisms often intimidated those around him; Clive Bell, Thoby's best friend, whose interest in art would lead him to marry Vanessa; Desmond MacCarthy, an attractive young man and a respected thinker who later became the leading literary critic of his generation; John Maynard Keynes, a brilliant economist, whose theories on markets and the government's role in the economy are still taught and debated; Roger Fry, the first English promoter of the then-unknown Post-Impressionist painters; E.M. Forster, a writer who became one of the twentieth century's leading novelists, composing such classics as *A Room with a View*, *Howard's End*, and *A Passage to India*; and Duncan Grant, who many considered the quintessential Bloomsbury artist. Woolf biographer Hermione Lee cites Leonard's list of Bloomsbury members: "Leonard Woolf, in the 1960s, listed 'Old Bloomsbury' as Vanessa and Clive Bell, Virginia and Leonard Woolf, Adrian and Karin Stephen, Lytton Strachey, Roger Fry, Desmond and Molly MacCarthy, with Julian, Quentin and Angelica Bell, and David Garnett as later additions. Other lists might include Ottoline Morrell, or Dora Carrington, or James and Alix Strachey." (Lee, 259) Clearly, "the Bloomsbury Group" is a loose label for a large circle of friends and acquaintances.

The son of Woolf's friend Vita Sackville-West later described a typical gathering:

> The room was large, smoky and warmed more by excitement than by artificial means. There were divans and carpets, walls painted gaudily ... gramophone records on trays and books everywhere. People were sitting on the floor at other people's feet, and there was much noise and laughter. . . . People were jumping up all the time, reaching for a book, peering at a picture. There was an undercurrent of competitiveness, as if everyone had to justify his presence each time afresh. (Nicolson, 36)

As a group, they were more open and honest about relationships and sex than the culture they grew up in, and the men treated women as equals. They respected intellectual excellence and believed in working hard for it. They accepted many behaviors and lifestyles and regarded homosexuality as normal. The group represented a new lifestyle and cultivated a contempt for sheer moneymaking and the status it brought — they refused to wear expensive clothes, instead spending their money on travel and art. They believed in sheer fun and laughter in all its forms. They were suspicious of power and its uses and were life-long pacifists when much of the rest of the world was at war. Some scholars have suggested that their greatest contribution was their concept of friendship, as once they became friends, nothing parted them for the rest of their lives — not war, age, success, or separation. E.M. Forster stated that if he had to choose between betraying his country and his friends, he hoped he would have the courage to betray his country.

However, they were not saints. They were often abrasive and reduced more than one visitor to tears as they ripped his or her ideas or arguments to shreds. They had no trouble excluding others; if they found guests boring, they were not invited back. The group was indifferent to science and religion and could be superficial as they replaced one set of beliefs with another. Some people hated them, seeing them only as destroyers of morals. They were in many senses the forerunners of the counterculture of the 1960s and provoked the same strong passions that the hippie lifestyle did.

Without deference to London's strict social conventions, the Stephen sisters also joined the intellectual gatherings.

FROM *A ROOM OF ONE'S OWN*

A Room of One's Own (1929) is considered one of Woolf's key works and the first major feminist essay in Western literature. It began as an address entitled "Women and Fiction," to be given at two women's colleges at Cambridge; Woolf wrote the address in May of 1928 and delivered it in October. In this essay, she explores the differences between the male and female academic facilities and access to education, asking why so few female writers are represented in the Western literary tradition. In the following passage, Woolf discusses the troubling instability of the female figure in history and male-written literature:

. . . [I]f woman had no existence save in the fiction written by men, one would imagine her a person of the utmost importance; very various; heroic and mean; splendid and sordid; infinitely beautiful and hideous in the extreme; as great as a man, some think even greater. But this is woman in fiction. In fact . . . she was locked up, beaten and flung about the room. A very queer, composite being thus emerges. Imaginatively she is of the highest importance; practically she is completely insignificant. She pervades poetry from cover to cover; she is all but absent from history.

royalty from Abyssinia, Woolf, Adrian, and four friends sent the navy a telegram stating their desire to tour the navy's newest and most prestigious battleship, the *Dreadnought*. They met with a costume designer who provided the friends with the clothing and makeup necessary for their disguises. Woolf, the only female participant, wore an embroidered caftan with chains and a turban. In addition, she used a beard and mustache to cover her blackened face.

On February 10, 1910, the "Abyssinian" entourage arrived in Weymouth, where the British Navy met them. With Adrian acting as a translator (using mispronounced phrases of Virgil and Homer), the six friends toured the ship. Upon their return, Horace leaked the prank to the newspapers. The navy was outraged to discover the deception. The *Dreadnought*'s flag commander was especially upset by the charade, as he was none other than the Stephens' cousin William Fisher. The joke angered many people and led to discussions in Parliament about tightening security around warships. Though few people caught its political and pacifist significance, the prank brought the Bloomsbury Group its first publicity. It also left a lasting impression on Woolf as an example of "masculine honor, of masculine violence and stupidity, of gold-laced masculine pomposity." (Leaska, 114) Years later, Woolf would incorporate her memory of the navy's stiff protocol into her feminist essays— specifically *Three Guineas*. The *Dreadnought* Hoax marked the start of a period of great personal growth for Woolf.

The Author Matures

1910–1913

One of the signs of passing youth is the birth of a sense of fellowship with other human beings as we take our place among them.
— Virginia Woolf, "Hours in a Library" (1916)

EMERGING IDEAS

As Woolf's circle of friends grew, so too did her social skills. She tried hard to overcome her natural shyness and was even the hit of a scandalous ball thrown in the fall of 1910. Her friend Roger Fry had arranged for several unknown artists to show their work at the Grafton Galleries. Both the First Post-Impressionist Exhibition (as it was called) and the ball that accompanied it shocked the art world. Some art critics considered the work by these new artists—Cézanne, Van Gogh, Matisse, and Picasso—"pornographic . . . the work of madmen"; many ridiculed the paintings, some were amused,

Leonard Woolf and Virginia Stephen, 1912. After his long
and determined pursuit, Leonard Woolf married Virginia
Stephen. From their first meeting almost a decade earlier
and through seven years of separation, each held affections
and hopes for the other. As her sister Vanessa would write,
Leonard was the only man she (or Virginia, for that matter)
could think of as Virginia's husband; in fact, Virginia rejected
many pursuits and proposals from other men before accepting
Leonard's in 1912. This photograph was taken at the time
of their engagement.

and a few appreciated the new art direction. (Nicolson, 43) Woolf was moved by the paintings and realized that she wanted to write in the same style in which these artists painted. She decided that her writings should illuminate the essence of people, objects, and relationships without attempting to recreate them. The ball celebrating the exhibition was a large gathering, and Vanessa and Woolf attended the festivities wearing bare-shouldered gowns (almost the equivalent of a see-through dress today). Several guests thought the sisters were under the influence of fleeting French fashions, and others were too shocked to comment. Needless to say, the notoriety of the Bloomsbury Group continued to grow after the ball.

Woolf's political awareness began to grow as well. In 1910, she joined the women's suffrage movement and spent many hours stuffing envelopes in support of women's right to vote in political elections. Woolf thought political activism was foolish, though, and took no further role in the women's movement after women obtained the right to vote in 1918. However, her commitment to women's rights remained strong and became a common theme in her writing. Through her novels and essays, Woolf supported her belief that women's values and skills were too often ignored by society. Her works argued not for equal rights, but for recognition that women and men have different strengths and values. Given these differences, Woolf felt that civic life should include input from both sexes.

With her ideas maturing, Woolf's thoughts turned to marriage. She had many suitors of varying talents and qualifications, but few could hold her interest. She flirted with Walter Headlam, a poet, Greek scholar, and Hellenist who was old enough to be her father; their courtship was cut short when he died in 1908. After that, she turned down proposals from Walter Lamb and Sydney Waterlow and discouraged attentions from Saxon Sydney-Turner and Edward Hilton Young, stating that she would marry no one but Lytton Strachey. When Lytton proposed on February 17, 1909, Woolf accepted his proposal immediately—only to change her mind minutes later, to her own and Strachey's relief. Strachey, who was openly homosexual, corresponded regularly with Woolf. They enjoyed each other's wit and humor, and the "safety" of Strachey's homosexuality may have attracted the sexually inexperienced Woolf. (A peripheral Bloomsbury member, the painter Dora Carrington, established what seems to have been a very loving relationship with Strachey that lasted almost two decades; she committed suicide soon after his death.)

A MARRIAGE OF MINDS

In 1911, the lease of 29 Fitzroy Square ended, and Woolf and Adrian moved to a four-story house located at 38 Brunswick Square. They rented the extra space to their friends: Duncan Grant and Maynard Keynes shared the ground floor, Adrian was on the second floor, Virginia lived on the third floor, and Leonard Woolf, having just returned from his seven-year service in Ceylon, resided on the fourth floor. This living situation was unusual for the time, and many Bloomsbury outsiders considered it scandalous—it was not socially acceptable for a woman, especially an unmarried woman, to live with men.

During his absence from Bloomsbury, Leonard had become a magistrate of a British territory and had developed a fascination for politics. He had also harbored the hope that Virginia might marry him. Although they did not correspond during his absence from Bloomsbury, Lytton Strachey's letters (following Strachey's own proposal) had encouraged Leonard to pursue her. Upon his return to England, the Bloomsbury friends welcomed Leonard as a dark and mysterious addition to their group. He was included in their gatherings and developed many new friendships.

Woolf enjoyed Leonard's company. She frequently invited him to her country residence at Asheham House in Sussex Downs, where they went for long walks. Their friendship grew, and Leonard fell in love with Virginia. She turned down his initial marriage proposal in January of 1912, but Vanessa encouraged him to keep trying: "You're the only person I know whom I can imagine as her husband." (Leaska, 154) By the spring, Leonard felt sufficiently reassured of her feelings that he resigned from Colonial Service to remain in England with her.

Virginia hesitated to accept Leonard's proposals, because she feared that her unstable mental health would burden him. She also worried that she could not reciprocate the depth of his feelings for her, stating, "I feel angry sometimes at the strength of your desire." (Nicolson, 48) To her, Leonard was difficult to love. He was Jewish, which, given her anti-Semitic upbringing, was somewhat objectionable. In addition, his hands trembled uncontrollably, and he often spilled his tea when he lifted a cup. Woolf wrote that this trembling had "moulded his life wrongly. All his shyness, his suffering from society, his sharpness and definiteness, might have been smoothed." (Nicolson, 48) Leonard persisted in his courting, and his support of her writing finally won her affection. On May 29, 1912, after a particularly fine lunch together, they became engaged.

Soon thereafter, Leonard arranged for Woolf to meet his family. The meeting did not go well; Virginia did not meet the expectations of Leonard's strong, matriarchal mother. But they were married anyway, in the middle of a violent thunderstorm on August 10, 1912. An elaborate church wedding would have been too conventional for the Bloomsbury Group, so the ceremony was short and simple and took place at the St. Pancras Registry Office. Vanessa and her family, Duncan Grant, George and Gerald Duckworth, Saxon Sydney-Turner, and Roger Fry were among those in attendance. Leonard's mother, who had found Woolf objectionable, was notably *not* present. Virginia was thirty years old and Leonard thirty-one.

THE HONEYMOON

After their wedding, the Woolfs traveled to France and Spain for their honeymoon, considering these countries more romantic

Roger Fry. An art critic and close friend of Woolf's since his joining the Bloomsbury Group in 1910, Fry was always the organizer, center, and life of the party. He even once arranged for then-unknown artistic giants like Van Gogh, Picasso, and Cézanne to display their work in conjunction with an avant-garde party thrown by the group. Bloomsbury regulars Duncan Grant, Dora Carrington, and Clive and Vanessa Bell, among others, also were visual artists, but it was Fry who incorporated the artistic revolution of the time into the equally rebellious work of the Bloomsbury Group. Woolf published a biography of Fry in 1940.

than their original destination, Iceland. The enchanting settings did nothing to promote their sexual intimacy, and by both of their accounts, their wedding night was a disappointment. Although Virginia loved Leonard, her sexual immaturity—possibly due to the abuse she had experienced as a child—seems to have prevented her from responding to him sexually. Instead, they clung to each other in long embraces for comfort and warmth. They were devoted and loving spouses, but most biographers believe that they were celibate for the duration of their thirty-year marriage. A decade later, on August 2, 1926, Woolf described in her diary the contrast that kept her marriage strong:

> [The British novelist] Arnold Bennett says that the horror of marriage lies in its "dailiness." All acuteness of relationship is rubbed away by this. The truth is more like this: life—say 4 days out of 7—becomes automatic; but on the 5th day a bead of sensation (between husband and wife) forms which is all the fuller and more sensitive because of the automatic customary unconscious days on either side. That is to say the year is marked by moments of great intensity. [Thomas] Hardy's "moments of vision." How can a relationship endure for any length of time except under these conditions? (A. Bell)

If the marriage was not fruitful, though, the honeymoon certainly *was*: the Woolfs returned with twin novels. His work, *The Village in the Jungle*, drew from his adventures in Ceylon, and hers was *Melymbrosia*, later renamed *The Voyage Out*. As she wrote in her diary in September of 1908, Woolf intended her novel to "achieve symmetry by means of infinite discords, showing all the traces of the mind's passage through the world; achieve at the end, some kind of whole made of shivering fragments." (Q. Bell) She was confident about her writing, and for a time, it soothed her. She wrote to her friend Violet Dickinson, "You can't think what an exquisite joy every minute of my life is to me now, and my only prayer is that I live to be 70." Attempting to capture her emotional explorations and sensory experiences, she revised *The Voyage Out* with terrific intensity. Upon its completion in March of 1913, she submitted the manuscript to her half-brother Gerald Duckworth's publishing company, where it was accepted enthusiastically. The novel was published two years later.

THE CYCLE BEGINS

Starting a cycle that would haunt her until her death, the anxiety brought on by the final revisions of her novel caused Woolf to once again "go mad." Her manuscript's acceptance triggered not joy, but sleepless nights, obsessive thoughts, headaches, and an aversion to food. Her depression and insanity deepened, and her family had to choose whether or not to certify her as insane.

Leonard, who may not have known the severity of Woolf's illnesses when he married her, sent her to a nursing home in Twickenham (near London), probably against her will. Doctors did their best to cure her, but her condition exceeded the skills and treatments of most physicians of the time. Even in her madness, Woolf recognized that Leonard and her siblings were trying to help her, and she worried about burdening them. She continued to send letters to her family and friends from the nursing home. Her letters to Leonard were affectionate and expressed her desire to recuperate from her illness: "I got up and dressed last night after you were gone, wanting to come back to you. You do represent all that's best, and I lie here thinking of you." (Nicolson, 55)

After three weeks in Twickenham, Leonard brought Woolf home to convalesce. He wanted to avoid institutionalizing her permanently and hoped that a comfortable environment with her family and friends close by would speed her recovery. Upon her return home, though, Woolf's mental health deteriorated once more. On September 8, 1913, a friend named Katherine ("Ka") Cox discovered Woolf unconscious in her bed after taking a near-fatal dose of the sleeping drug Veronal. Maynard Keynes's brother (a surgeon) was present at the time, and realizing the seriousness of her coma, rushed Woolf to St. Bartholomew's Hospital. Doctors pumped her stomach,

WOOLF ON ART IMITATING LIFE

Literary critics who study Woolf's work tend to look for similarities between her writing and events in her life. Some of these similarities are valid, but it is clear that Woolf did not like to see too much of an author in that author's work. In fact, Woolf criticized the celebrated British novelist George Eliot (1819–1880) for writing herself into her work too noticeably. The following excerpt is from Woolf's article "George Eliot," which first appeared in *The Times Literary Supplement* on November 20, 1919:

> [T]here are, even in the early works, traces of that troubled spirit, that exacting and questioning and baffled presence who was George Eliot herself. . . . Those who fall foul of George Eliot do so, we incline to think, on account of her heroines; and with good reason; for there is no doubt that they bring out the worst of her, lead her into difficult places, make her self-conscious, didactic, and occasionally vulgar. Yet if you could delete the whole sisterhood you would leave a much smaller and a much inferior world, albeit a world of greater artistic perfection and far superior jollity and comfort. In accounting for her failure, in so far as it was a failure, one recollects that she never wrote a story until she was thirty-seven, and that by the time she was thirty-seven she had come to think of herself with a mixture of pain and something like resentment. . . . Her self-consciousness is always marked when her heroines say what she herself would have said. She disguised them in every possible way. She granted them beauty and wealth into the bargain; she invented, more improbably, a taste for brandy. But the disconcerting and stimulating fact remained that she was compelled by the very power of her genius to step forth in person upon the quiet bucolic scene.

yet Woolf remained in a coma for two days. She awoke on the third day exhausted but alive. She recuperated slowly at Dalingridge Hall, George Duckworth's well-staffed mansion. Almost immediately following her recovery, Woolf began to work on her second novel, *Night and Day*.

5

The Road to Recovery

1914–1918

. . . [A] work of art is like a rose. A rose is not beautiful because it is like something else. Neither is a work of art. Roses and works of art are beautiful in themselves. Unluckily, the matter does not end there: a rose is the visible result of an infinitude of complicated goings on in the bosom of the earth and in the air above, and similarly a work of art is the product of strange activities in the human mind.

—Clive Bell, *Since Cézanne* (1922)

On the outskirts of every agony sits some observant fellow who points.

—Virginia Woolf, *The Waves* (1931)

CONSCIENTIOUS OBJECTORS

With Virginia's health improving, the Woolfs returned to Asheham in the summer of 1914—only to have World War I break out in August. They were initially unaffected by these world events. Leonard's trembling hands prevented him from serving in the

The studio at Charleston Farm. During World War I, many members of the group moved to a country house in Sussex, Charleston Farm, in protest. There they continued their meetings and continued producing their art. The studio, shown here, was added to the farmhouse in 1925 by Roger Fry. Various members of the group lived at Charleston— Clive and Vanessa Bell lived there for a while with Vanessa's lover, Duncan Grant, who also decorated the walls. The house still contains a number of furnishings from Woolf's childhood, as well as the table at which the lunch was eaten that Woolf describes in *A Room of One's Own* (1929).

armed forces, because the army worried that he would be a great danger to himself and others if he were to hold a rifle. As conscientious objectors, many of their Bloomsbury friends were also exempted from service. Most of them disagreed with war on moral grounds and denounced the government's use of war to achieve its political goals. Clive Bell, Vanessa's husband, published a pamphlet called *Peace at Once* that the mayor of London banned due to its defeatist arguments. Clive's pamphlet proposed that it was better to surrender than to lose more lives. Leonard disagreed, although he felt that England was fighting "a senseless and useless" war. (Nicolson, 59) Maynard Keynes also broke ranks with his Bloomsbury friends, declaring that war was necessary and should be conducted swiftly.

As an alternative to fighting, many members of the Bloomsbury Group took to farming. The Bell family, Duncan Grant, and David Garnett relocated to a large farmhouse called Charleston, where they worked for the duration of the war. With its members spread out, the Bloomsbury Group found its regular meeting schedule difficult to maintain. Woolf wrote that she regretted that the parties had "vanished like the morning mist." She missed her friends, although the separation helped strengthen her relationship with Leonard.

Woolf wrote very little about World War I in her diary or letters and disregarded it as much as possible. She considered that wars were symptomatic of a male-dominated society, "a preposterous masculine fiction" that made men seem like a separate and foreign, primitive culture. (Nicolson, 58) She heard gunfire from France at her country home and slept in the cellar to escape air raids, but these events went unrecorded in her journals and correspondence. Images from the war appeared in several of her later works though, including *Jacob's Room* and *The Years*.

Woolf's mental stability fluctuated for the first two years of the war. During a period of lucidity, she and Leonard discovered and fell in love with a beautiful house in Richmond called Hogarth House. Her clarity did not last long, however, and in February of 1915 she suffered possibly her worst episode of mental illness. Leonard described it as "a nightmare world of frenzy, despair, and violence." (Nicolson, 56) He was unable to help her, and it was not until September of 1915 that she resumed her slow recovery.

LIFE GOES ON

The Woolfs found that their new country house was an idyllic place, with a hundred-foot garden and beautiful trees. To speed Woolf's rehabilitation, Leonard enforced a strict daily routine:

They wrote in the morning, went for long afternoon walks, and read in the evening. Once or twice a week, they ventured to London to conduct business, shop, attend concerts, and visit friends. Woolf took Italian lessons, and Leonard became more involved with politics.

Although she was not keen on politics, Woolf attended a few of Leonard's political gatherings, contributing her opinions when appropriate. She became an active member of the Richmond branch of the Women's Co-operative Guild. As chair, she held monthly meetings that featured guest speakers who presented progressive perspectives on several women's issues, including women's roles in the armed forces, the dangers of venereal disease, and the war's effects on young soldiers. These topics shocked the organization's members. For the four years Woolf served in the guild, she always upheld her choice of controversial speakers and subjects. She felt that women needed to be informed about all issues that affected them, and she failed to understand women who chose to remain ignorant.

Woolf's daily writing schedule helped increase her output, and she was extremely prolific in the years following her mental collapse in 1915. By 1917, she was consistently writing reviews, essays, and short stories for *The Times Literary Supplement*, *The Athenaeum*, and *The New Statesmen*. In an article entitled "Modern Fiction," she criticized the respected novelists of the day, including H.G. Wells, Arnold Bennett, and John Galsworthy, calling them "materialists" who were concerned not with the spirit but with the body of characters. Instead, she considered that writers should "examine . . . an ordinary mind on an ordinary day." She suggested a new writing style was necessary to capture the mind's "myriad [of] impressions," that if a writer "could write what he chose, not what he must, if he could base his work upon his own feeling and not upon convention, there would be no plot, no comedy, no tragedy, no love interest or catastrophe in the accepted style." In short, "Modern Fiction" provided an overview of her new approach to storytelling, one that she would develop further in many of her future novels. (Lehmann, 46)

CRITICAL ACCLAIM

After several delays caused by her illness, the uncertainties of war, and various moves, Woolf's first book was released on March 26, 1915. *The Voyage Out* received excellent reviews, and she was labeled a genius. E.M. Forster even compared the novel to Emily Brontë's classic *Wuthering Heights*. Woolf herself always feared that her work was "an idiot's dream, of no value to anyone," and these accolades reassured her. Despite the book's critical acclaim, though, it saw very little commercial success. *The Voyage Out* made less than £125 for its author.

Centered on a young woman, *The Voyage Out* tells the story of Rachel Vinrace's trip to South America. Accompanied by her father, Rachel visits her aunt in Santa Marina. While she is there, she falls in love with a novelist named Terence Hewitt. Rachel is a talented pianist, but the authority figures in her life (including her father and Terence) discourage her musical abilities. As a result, she loses her ability to express herself through her performances. Despite their differences, Rachel and Terence become engaged, but Rachel falls ill and dies before they can marry.

Critics consider *The Voyage Out* to be a conventional story of a young woman coming of age. The novel proceeds in time sequentially from beginning to end, and the plot and characters build until resolution occurs when Rachel dies at the end of the story. Still, this poetic novel contains many aspects of Woolf's future masterpieces: the natural beauty of the world, the appreciation of history, the novelty of foreign travel, and the examination of the meaning of life and marriage.

THE HOGARTH PRESS

As life at Hogarth House settled into a rhythm, the Woolfs sought further diversion from their work. They enjoyed their walks and trips to London, but their considerable energy turned their thoughts to publishing. The Woolfs were not prosperous, and they hoped that printing would provide additional income, as well as serve as a distraction. After some thought, they purchased a small printing press for less than £20 on March 23, 1917. It was a wise choice. With some help from a local printer, the Woolfs set the block of type, inked the press, and published their first booklet, *Two Stories*, a month later. The 32-page booklet contained two short stories, one from each of them. They printed 150 copies, which they sold to family and friends for 1s.6d. each. The Hogarth Press was on its way.

In 1917, the war that had seemed so distant finally became

WOOLF ON GEORGE ELIOT'S DIALOGUE

In her 1919 *Times Literary Supplement* article on George Eliot, Woolf provides her own opinions on dialogue by contrasting Eliot's skill with Jane Austen's. Mrs. Casaubon is a character in Eliot's most respected novel, *Middlemarch* (1871–1872), which Woolf refers to as "the magnificent book which with all its imperfections is one of the few English novels written for grown-up people." Emma and Knightley are characters in Austen's *Emma* (1815).

> . . . [H]er [Eliot's] hold upon dialogue, when it is not dialect, is slack; and . . . she seems to shrink with an elderly dread of fatigue from the effort of emotional concentration. She allows her heroines to talk too much. She has little verbal felicity. She lacks the unerring taste which chooses one sentence and compresses the heart of the scene within that. 'Whom are you going to dance with?' asked Mr Knightley, at the Weston's ball. 'With you, if you will ask me,' said Emma; and she has said enough. Mrs Casaubon would have talked for an hour and we should have looked out of the window.

a daily concern. Air raids occurred each month with the full moon, and the Woolfs and their visitors were forced to stay in the basement at Hogarth House. Leonard slept on a table with Woolf below, while others shared bunks. Woolf showed great courage during the air raids. She often made jokes to lift everyone's spirits and keep people distracted until the raids were over. These jests began to bother Leonard, who finally demanded that she stop. One of his brothers was killed in the war and another wounded, and he was devastated by the violence. As the war was winding down in the spring of 1918, the raids became less frequent. The full moon was no longer a source of dread, though Woolf noted that the spring sunshine that year had an unhealthy and strange coloring and seemed like no spring light before or after.

Through it all, printing became a constant source of happiness and frustration for both Woolf and Leonard. They found the work rewarding, but the time commitment it required was often overwhelming. Woolf organized the type, because Leonard's trembling hands disrupted the many small metal pieces. She arranged the letters on a printer's rule for hours, allowing Leonard to review her work at the end of every fifth line. Leonard operated the press itself. They could print only two pages at a time, as they lacked the type for more. After printing two pages, Woolf would rework the inky type for the next two pages. Woolf wrote, "You can't think how exciting, soothing, ennobling, and satisfying it is." (Nicolson, 64) The process was tedious, but the Woolfs found their handiwork therapeutic. Perhaps most exciting was that it gave Woolf the freedom to publish her works herself.

The Hogarth Press made a small profit from the start. The Woolfs paid themselves nothing for their labor, and the cost of materials was not high. Like the owners of many small businesses, they soon required an assistant. The first assistant they hired was a neighbor named Barbara Hiles, whom they paid in hot meals on the days she worked. With her help, the

Hogarth Press grew busier. It began to accept avant-garde poems and stories that other publishers avoided.

The third work the Hogarth Press published was written by a talented young female writer whom the Woolfs had met some years earlier. Attracted by her early stories, Woolf pursued Katherine Mansfield to submit a story to the press. Katherine offered them a 68-page story called *Prelude.* It was a large undertaking for the press. Woolf set all the type herself, and together she and Leonard bound, marketed, and distributed the story themselves. It sold 247 copies.

Woolf and Katherine Mansfield shared a dubious friendship, based mainly on their competitiveness as writers. They spoke about literature and were genial together, but apart they were highly critical of each other's work. Woolf found *Prelude* "vapourish . . . and fully watered with some of her cheap realities." (Leaska, 200) Nevertheless, the story conveyed the thoughts of a serious writer. Woolf considered Mansfield her main rival, as Mansfield's approach to fiction was so similar to her own. Both women were transforming fiction with their indirect storytelling, subtle, thoughtful characters, and reliance on visual imagery. Despite their mutual animosity, Woolf was grieved to hear of Mansfield's death in 1923 from tuberculosis. She wrote, "a rival the less," but "it seemed to me that there is no point in writing: Katherine won't read it." (Nicolson, 75) Over the years, their relationship had sparked creativity and often anger, and Woolf missed her rival.

After *Prelude,* the Hogarth Press continued to find and publish works from promising writers and poets. On May 12, 1919, the Woolfs published a collection of poetry by an unknown American expatriate named T.S. Eliot. E.M. Forster's *The Story of the Siren* followed in 1920. Almost overnight, the Hogarth Press grew from a hobby into a real business.

As demand for their work grew, the Woolfs invested in larger, more state-of-the-art equipment. In 1921, they purchased a pedal-driven press. Soon after, they published Eliot's

Katherine Mansfield. Mansfield was one of the first authors whose work was published by the Hogarth Press. She was Woolf's literary rival, and the two shared a critical respect for each other, perhaps tinged by a bit of jealousy on Mansfield's part. Mansfield's work spurred Woolf on in healthy competition to write more and better stories, and when Mansfield died in 1923, Woolf felt the loss of a great peer and critic. Woolf even mused that it was not worth writing books anymore because Mansfield was not there to read them.

The Waste Land, one of the most influential works in both American and British literature. As with many groundbreaking works, *The Waste Land* did not enjoy much initial success. In the first six months, the Hogarth Press sold only 330 copies, to the disappointment of both the author and publisher. The Woolfs were also offered James Joyce's *Ulysses,* which they declined. They considered the length of the manuscript too daunting for their little publishing house. Even with the new equipment, it would have taken them two years to set the type. In addition, Woolf found Joyce's experimental fiction disagreeable.

"Never did I read such tosh," she wrote to Lytton Strachey on April 24, 1922. "As for the first two chapters we will let them pass, but the 3rd 4th 5th 6th—merely the scratching of pimples on the body of the bootboy at Claridges." (Nicolson)

Most Bloomsbury authors were under contract to large publishers and did not use the Hogarth Press. Others, such as Eliot, Forster, and William Plomer, abandoned Hogarth for larger publishing houses once they became famous. By 1930, the Hogarth Press made £2,373 with the release of Vita Sackville-West's *The Edwardians*, and in 1937 it made £2,442 on Virginia Woolf's *The Years*.

The Hogarth Press remains a publishing legend to this day. During Woolf's lifetime alone, the press published 474 books, including nine of her own works, eight translations of Freud, and the Eliot volumes. The press published a number of very important psychoanalytical works in addition to Freud's. Later, in his memoirs, Leonard recalled Freud: "The greatest pleasure that I got from publishing The Psycho-Analytical Library was the relationship which it established between us and Freud. . . . Nearly all famous men are disappointing or bores, or both. Freud was neither; he had an aura, not of fame, but of greatness." (Woolf, *Downhill All the Way*) The Hogarth Press was the main source of psychoanalytic theory in England at the time.

The Woolfs developed a love/hate relationship with their success. "It's worse than six children at the breast simultaneously," wrote Woolf to a friend. (Nicolson, 66) However, it liberated Virginia, allowing her "to be able to do what one likes—no editors, or publishers, and only people to read who more or less like that sort of thing." The Hogarth Press enabled her to escape her dependence on Gerald Duckworth, so that neither she nor her work would be "pawed and snored over" by a man she disliked. Having her own press also freed her from "Victorian, conventional, anti-experimental" publishers. From the start, the Hogarth Press embodied anti-Victorian, unconventional, experimental publishing—a market that it helped create.

6

Finding Her Voice

1918–1923

If we didn't live venturously, plucking the wild goat by the beard, and trembling over precipices, we should never be depressed, I've no doubt; but already should be faded, fatalistic and aged.

—Virginia Woolf, diary, May 26, 1924, quoted in *A Writer's Diary*, ed. Leonard Woolf

NIGHT AND DAY

November of 1918 brought an end to Woolf's second novel, *Night and Day*, which, unlike *The Voyage Out*, caused her no anguish to complete. In fact, she said, "I've never enjoyed any writing so much as I did the last half of *Night and Day*." (Nicolson, 68) Having begun the novel during her recovery, she composed much of it while lying in bed on doctor's orders. She wrote, "I was so tremblingly afraid of my own insanity that I wrote *Night and Day* mainly to prove to my own satisfaction

Monk's House. The Woolfs bought Monk's House, on the River Ouse in East Sussex, in 1919. They spent mainly their summers there until their house in London was bombed out in 1940. The house, about ten miles away from Charleston Farm, provided the couple with an atmosphere suitable to their simplistic and laid-back lifestyle, as well as a place of refuge from the constant tension of air-raid sirens and war. Free from these stressors, both Virginia and Leonard began to explore their passions and art with even greater fervor. Leonard even took up gardening, a hobby he would cherish for the rest of his life. Virginia's ashes are interred at Monk's House.

that I could keep entirely off that dangerous ground." The result was a leisurely novel that lacked the poetic visionary quality that would become her trademark.

Night and Day follows a young heroine named Katharine who must resolve her feelings about her marriage, her family, and her work. She is older and stronger than Rachel, the main character of *The Voyage Out*; and, unlike Rachel, Katharine survives the story. She desires an escape from her restrictive home life, but she understands the inherent contradiction in her quest for happiness: Katharine craves independence, but she believes her life's fulfillment can only be found in an intimate relationship. In seeking solitude, she discovers that she can achieve happiness in the company of another. As the novel progresses, Katharine realizes that she can enjoy her marriage and lead a fulfilling life. Unlike Rachel, when Katharine finds her voice in the language of mathematics, she is not pressured to discontinue her self-expression. Although she does wonder what her life might have been like had she not married, the story reaches a happy conclusion, with Katharine and her husband working through the compromises of marriage. Interestingly, neither Rachel nor Katharine likes to read—Woolf's lifelong passion. The following passage from *Night and Day* illustrates the degree to which Woolf's fiction stood independent of the social codes of its day and considered the "game" of life from a less biased perspective. The meditative, introspective feel of the text is common in Woolf's work:

> As she put her hat on she determined to lunch at a shop in the Strand, so as to set that other piece of mechanism, her body, into action. With a brain working and a body working one could keep step with the crowd and never be found out for the hollow machine, lacking the essential thing, that one was conscious of being.
>
> She considered her case as she walked down the Charing Cross Road. She put to herself a series of questions. Would she mind, for example, if the wheels of that motor-omnibus passed over her and crushed her to death? No, not in the least; or an adventure with that disagreeable-looking man hanging about the entrance of the Tube station? No; she could not conceive fear or excitement. Did suffering in any form appall her? No, suffering was neither good nor bad. And this essential thing? In the eyes of every single person she detected a flame; as if a spark in the brain ignited spontaneously at contact with the things they met and drove them on.

Gerald Duckworth published *Night and Day* on October 20, 1919. With few exceptions, the reviews were excellent. Perhaps with some jealousy, Katherine Mansfield declared that she hated it, stating that in *Night and Day* Woolf failed to acknowledge the changes the war had brought to the world. E.M. Forster also criticized the book, as he found none of the characters lovable. In spite of these criticisms, the novel advanced Woolf's career and increased her growing reputation as a talented new writer. To Woolf's dismay, though, the book made more money for its publisher than it did for its author.

The Woolfs' finances were generally limited. Leonard wrote about international politics regularly and worked as an editor for *The International Review* for a short time, but his fees and salary were minimal. The Hogarth Press netted only £90 in its first four years of operation, and Woolf earned about £100 each year on her journalism projects. Still, they managed to maintain a house in Bloomsbury and a house in the country for the duration of their marriage. They also rented three cottages in Cornwall for £15 a year and purchased and sold several properties, including Hogarth House and another called Round House. After selling Round House, the Woolfs bought a summer cottage called Monk's House, which remained their country home for the rest of their lives.

MONK'S HOUSE

The Woolfs purchased Monk's House for £700 around the same time that *Night and Day* was published. The plain cottage was the last house on a pretty lane that ended near a river, and the Woolfs enjoyed peace and solitude whenever they stayed there. When they moved in, the cottage lacked running water, electricity, and a bath, and its garden was an overgrown jungle. The house was damp and uncomfortable, but Woolf appreciated its simplicity. She and Leonard also loved the cottage's orchard. They made improvements on the house when time and money permitted, and the backyard jungle inspired Leonard to pursue gardening, a hobby he enjoyed for the remainder of his life. From the house, they could look across the valley, and the only sounds that disturbed their quiet were the tolling church bells and the cries of children from the nearby school—welcome changes from the war's air-raid sirens.

MODERNISM IN LITERATURE

As a writer, Woolf is generally considered a Modernist. The roots of Modernism can be found in the mid-nineteenth century, but Modernism in literature was born around the time of World War I. It was at this time that the nineteenth-century notion of Progress—that throughout history God had directed human spiritual, social, and technological development toward the inevitable perfection of mankind—was breaking down. The "unsinkable" R.M.S. *Titanic*, a triumph of early-twentieth-century shipbuilding, had sunk catastrophically in 1912. World War I, which Europe had expected to be relatively brief and painless, and to which some had been looking forward as a relief from international tensions, became savage, bloody, and horrific. At the same time, the psychoanalyst Sigmund Freud was writing about sex and aggression for increasingly large audiences, and, following Charles Darwin's work, humans were being studied as one might study animals. All these factors, with many others, led intellectuals to wonder whether humans really were improving, or whether Progress had been nothing more than a beautiful lie that could no longer be supported.

It was in this climate that literary Modernism was born. Modernist works tend to express themes of fragmentation, loss, and uncertainty, as well as subjectivity—the sense that every person is fundamentally alone and that emotions and

The Woolfs were never known to keep an immaculate house, and Monk's House's shabby, relaxed setting did not provide a motivation for tidiness. Friends reported that books were often piled on the stairs and saucers of pet food covered the floor. Neither Woolf nor Leonard had an eye for decoration or for architecture; the annex Leonard built for Woolf's

impressions of the world cannot be communicated with any accuracy. Woolf's *Mrs. Dalloway* and *To the Lighthouse* are considered among the premiere works of Modernist fiction, as are works of James Joyce (especially *Ulysses*), Franz Kafka, Thomas Mann, Gertrude Stein, Marcel Proust, T.S. Eliot, Ezra Pound, Katherine Mansfield, D.H. Lawrence, and William Faulkner.

The Bloomsbury Group and the Woolfs' Hogarth Press became closely associated with the movement. Leonard, Vita Sackville-West, and others prepared and published several important original translations of foreign works, including those of Tolstoy, Dostoevsky, and Rainer Maria Rilke. Hogarth published a volume of Eliot's poems in 1921, when he was working on "The Love Song of J. Alfred Prufrock." In 1924, the Press began to publish the papers of the International Psycho-Analytical Institute — and thereby became Freud's official publisher in England. Following Pound's advice, the Modernists tried to destroy old literary forms and create new ones. Woolf herself wrote in 1924, "On or about December 1910 human character changed. All human relations shifted — those between masters and servants, husbands and wives, parents and children. And when human relations shift there is at the same time a change in religion, conduct, politics, and literature." ("Mr. Bennett and Mrs. Brown") bedroom was poorly designed and lacked direct access from the house. In addition, the furniture they chose was unappealing. The only objects of interest were Vanessa's painted tiles that surrounded the fireplaces and a set of tables and chairs created by Roger Fry's friends. The house's modest appearance paid tribute to the Bloomsbury Group's desire for truth and simplicity rather than luxury and comfort. Both Charleston (Vanessa's home) and Monk's House are closely identified with Bloomsbury and still exist in their restored conditions.

THE NEW CELEBRITY

Soon after moving to Monk's House, Woolf began work on her third novel, *Jacob's Room.* This novel represented her first full-length experiment with fiction. In it, she abolished the traditional elements of a novel, including the plot and narrator. Instead, she used each character to describe the behavior of other characters and advanced the story through a series of quick, impressionistic events. Woolf wrote that the book "had some merit, but it's too much of an experiment." However, her diary indicates that she was excited about the breakthroughs she had made with her book: "I have found out how to begin (at 40) to say something in my own voice." On October 27, 1922, *Jacob's Room* became the first full-length book published by the Hogarth Press.

Jacob's Room focuses on the life of Jacob Flanders, presenting images of his childhood, his university life, his travels, his loves, and his death during World War I. The narrative is out of sequence, and the story is told by several women who knew Jacob, including his mother, Betty Flanders. The glimpses of Jacob's life describe his character indirectly, but Woolf hoped that they revealed his true personality.

Jacob's Room made Woolf a celebrity. Her bold writing experiment shocked critics, who were afraid to judge the book too harshly for fear that they misunderstood a masterpiece. She was hailed as a wonderful new talent and became the talk of

The garden house. The annex Leonard built for Woolf as her writing studio at Monk's House was far from ideal, but it gave Woolf a "room of her own" that she truly cherished and where she wrote diligently on her characteristic blue paper. In keeping with the theme of the main house, Woolf's annex was a place of relaxed (and disorganized) comfort—an atmosphere perfectly suited for the pursuit of her art.

England's literary community. She found her life changed, filled with invitations to celebrity parties and speaking engagements. She called these outings her "social adventures" and joked about the number of invitations she received each day. She disliked people with "a slipperiness of the soul," those socialites who were insincere and untruthful. In addition, she learned to despise people who tried to impress her with their knowledge of literature or politics. Such people became objects of her sharp tongue and quick wit.

PEACE ATTAINED

Always shy in social situations, Woolf preferred to attend parties with children and joined their games without self-consciousness. She loved her nieces and nephews and was a popular aunt. She struck one of her nephews as a wonderful tall bird, whose clothes were like folded wings. When they knew she was coming to visit, Vanessa's children would compose their own plays and perform them for Woolf's amusement. In turn, she would question them on the details of their lives. She asked them which sock they put on first in the morning and whether they thought the sun looked happy or sad. Nevertheless, the Woolfs agreed not to have children of their own. In December of 1927, she wrote in her diary:

> The little creatures acting moved my infinitely senti-
> mental throat. Angelica so mature and composed; all
> grey and silver; such an epitome of all womanliness;
> and such an unopened bud of sense and sensibility;
> wearing a grey wig and a sea-coloured dress. And yet
> oddly enough I scarcely want children of my own now.
> This insatiable desire to write something before I die,
> this ravaging sense of the shortness and feverishness of
> life, make me cling, like a man on a rock, to my one
> anchor. I don't like the physicalness of having children
> of one's own. (Lehmann, 71)

Having become a well-known author, Woolf appreciated her solitude more than ever. She claimed that she was happiest when she was alone. However, her success promoted her self-confidence, and she was often the life of social gatherings. Her conversations were lively, overflowing with unpredictable questions, fantasies, and laughter.

Her new fame seems to have helped her home life, too. Apart, she and Leonard wrote to each other every day, and she called him her "precious beast." Leonard's political and literary exploits had advanced his career as well. In March of 1923, he accepted an editorship with the *Nation*, and the Woolfs expressed their pride in each other's achievements. In addition, the Hogarth Press continued to find, publish, and market notable works, increasing their profits. Around Leonard, Woolf noted that she felt "entirely simple and sane."

With three novels written, and a fourth in its early stages, Woolf took some time to assess her beliefs on writing:

> But now what do I feel about my writing? . . . One must write from deep feeling, said Dostoievsky. And do I? Or do I fabricate with words, loving them as I do? No, I think not. . . . I want to give life and death, sanity and insanity; I want to criticize the social system, and show it at work, at its most intense. . . . I haven't that "reality" gift. I insubstantise, willfully to extent, distrusting reality— its cheapness. But to get further. Have I the power of conveying the true reality? Or do I write essays about myself? . . . I think it most important . . . to go for the central things. (Q. Bell, 2.99–100)

She decided that she needed to create memories for her characters to give them depth. She also realized that her writing required a new fluid style to convey people's thoughts, actions, and recollections. She wanted to capture the effects of scattered and random feelings, rather than focus on linear character

The favorite aunt. Although Virginia and Leonard Woolf never had children of their own, Virginia deeply loved her nieces and nephews, and she enjoyed playing games with them far more than she enjoyed social interaction with people her own age. The children in turn loved her and her obvious interest in their lives. Her involvement in their lives brought great fulfillment to them all. This photograph—of Virginia, Clive and Vanessa's daughter Angelica, Leonard, and a daughter of Virginia's friend Barbara Bagenal—was taken in the French town of Cassis, one of the Bloomsbury Group's summer retreats.

development to accomplish what she deemed "conveying the true reality."

Partly because of her position at the Hogarth Press, Woolf understood that the end of World War I and the beginning of the 1920s marked a new age of English literature. E.M. Forster, D.H. Lawrence, T.S. Eliot, Katherine Mansfield, and James Joyce were starting to redefine modern literary sensibilities. They were beginning to break the conventions of storytelling and poetry with fresh themes, fast narration, and unique, sophisticated characters. Little did Woolf know that her next three books would help lead this movement and that all her accomplishments to date were a minor prelude to her future masterpieces.

7

Woolf Becomes a Major Talent

1924–1931

. . . [W]hat a change of temper a fixed income will bring about[!] No force in the world can take from me my five hundred pounds. Food, house and clothing are mine for ever. Therefore not merely do effort and labour cease, but also hatred and bitterness. I need not hate any man; he cannot hurt me. I need not flatter any man; he has nothing to give me.

—Virginia Woolf, *A Room of One's Own* (1929)

RETURN TO BLOOMSBURY

In March of 1924, Woolf and Leonard decided to move back to Bloomsbury. They loved the peace of Hogarth House, but Leonard preferred to live closer to his business partners and Woolf missed her friends. In the years since the war, the Bloomsbury Group had reunited and thirteen of the friends gathered regularly to form the Memoir Club. The club's

Duncan Grant. When the Bloomsbury Group reunited after the war, their familiar culture was revived, but with new players and new arrangements. Marriages had shifted and broken, and lifestyles had altered. Vanessa had begun an affair with the Scottish-born painter and key Bloomsbury member Duncan Grant, whom Lytton Strachey also had admired. Grant was a painter of landscapes, portraits, and still-lifes; he decorated a number of Bloomsbury residences, including Charleston, where this photograph was taken in August of 1930.

purpose was to read and discuss their recollections of youth, although some said the recollections consisted more of fiction than of fact. The rest of the Bloomsbury Group continued to correspond among themselves, but many marriages and friendships had changed over time. Vanessa lived with her lover, Duncan Grant. Lytton Strachey lived with a woman who loved him, but he loved the woman's fiancé. Among their friends, only the Woolfs' marriage remained strong.

The Woolfs leased 52 Tavistock Square, a typical terrace house in Bloomsbury. They occupied the top two floors, rented the bottom two floors, and transferred the Hogarth Press to the basement. Using the press's stockroom as a writing room, Woolf resumed her work. She was constantly interrupted by the press's assistants, who required her help to answer phones, set type, and ship books. Despite these distractions, Woolf managed to complete her latest novel, *Mrs. Dalloway*.

Leonard was not surprised that she could work through these diversions, as Woolf's ability to concentrate was always amazing. When she wrote, her novels consumed her; even when she was not writing, her thoughts were on her work. Leonard began to worry that she could not rest, and he became concerned about her mental health. She still experienced intermittent blinding headaches and sleepless nights, but Woolf never felt sorry for herself or considered that she should stop writing. On the contrary, her writing became more experimental and her dedication to her novels grew.

MRS. DALLOWAY

Woolf began her fourth novel, *Mrs. Dalloway*, as early as 1920, developing most of the story between 1922 and 1924. The novel represented her continual experimentation with the conventions of fiction and introduced her new, more mature writing technique. To evolve characters with realistic thought and reactions, Woolf used the literary technique of "stream of consciousness" that was being developed by other Modernists. Stream of consciousness was Modernist writers' way of escaping from the linear structure of the novel; they wanted to focus not on narrating, on telling a story, but on their characters and the chaos of human thought. Using this technique enabled Woolf to capture her characters' personal feelings while effectively portraying the personalities of the others; by the end of the book, readers understand each character intimately. "The method of writing smooth narration can't be right," Woolf wrote. "Things don't happen in the mind like that. We experience, all the time, an overlapping of images and ideas, and modern novels should convey our mental confusion." (Nicolson, 96) She wanted her novels to portray the true experiences of life, and she realized that sensations and perceptions provided the ingredients to create this fictional reality. In her diary, in August of 1924, she wrote, "I want the concentration & the romance, & the words all glued together, fused, glowing: have no time to waste any more on prose." (A. Bell)

Mrs. Dalloway is about a single day—possibly June 20, 1923—in the lives of several people as they travel in and through London. It contrasts the preparations for Clarissa Dalloway's party with the madness of the war survivor Septimus Warren-Smith. Acting as foils for each other, Clarissa and Septimus examine the sacrifices of their lives from opposite ends of the social spectrum. Both seek solace in death as an escape from the futility of life, although only Septimus commits suicide. Much of the action occurs in the characters' minds, and only once does Woolf break the flow of the narration to offer commentary on the characters. *Mrs. Dalloway* swells with emotionally charged poetic images, and Woolf considered it a celebration of her beloved London.

The response to *Mrs. Dalloway* following its publication in April of 1925 was mixed. Both critics and readers were confused by the novel's unconventional approach to plot, narration, and setting. Woolf noted that few people seemed to understand her intention. Regardless, *Mrs. Dalloway* contributed to her growing reputation, as readers sensed Woolf's impact on English literature.

TO THE LIGHTHOUSE

Woolf's next novel, *To the Lighthouse*, is considered one of her best and among the most typical of her style and her contribution to Western literature. No description of its creation—and its importance in her own life—can match her own. She included the following passage in the autobiographical "A Sketch from the Past" (1938):

> Until I was in the forties—I could settle the date by seeing when I wrote *To the Lighthouse*, but am too casual here to bother to do it—the presence of my mother obsessed me. I could hear her voice, see her, imagine what she would do or say as I went about my day's doings. She was one of the invisible presences who after all play so important a part in every life. . . .
>
> Then one day walking round Tavistock Square I made up, as I sometimes make up my books, *To the Lighthouse*, in a great, apparently involuntary, rush. One thing burst into another. . . . I wrote the book very quickly; and when it was written, I ceased to be obsessed by my mother. I no longer hear her voice; I do not see her.
>
> I suppose that I did for myself what psycho-analysts do for their patients. I expressed some very long felt and deeply felt emotion. And in expressing it I explained it and then laid it to rest. But what is the meaning of 'explained' it? (Schulkind, 80–81)

Excited by her new writing style, Woolf worked on the novel feverishly until, in the summer of 1925, she collapsed. Her long hours at the press, multiple social engagements, and continuous stream of creativity had exhausted her. Her weakened condition persisted into 1926, and she was forced to rest, setting her writing and other duties aside. When her health had recovered enough for her to resume work, she found that her writing was fluid and easy. "Never," she noted, "have I written so easily, imagined so profusely." (Lehmann, 55) This enjoyment of writing did not last long, though, and by the completion of the manuscript Woolf saw herself as "an elderly dowdy fussy ugly incompetent woman; vain, chattering, and futile."

To the Lighthouse takes place in the fictional village of Finlay, on the Isle of Skye, and draws heavily on the happy experiences of the Stephen family at St. Ives. The novel's main characters reflect Leslie and Julia Stephen, with Mr. Ramsey, the insecure, yet arrogant philosopher, and Mrs. Ramsey, the active, dedicated, and submissive mother. The story moves in three segments that span a ten-year period extending through and after World War I. The first segment shows an afternoon and evening in the life of the vacationing Ramsey family. The next propels the reader forward in time, with mild references to the changes occurring within the six or seven years that pass by. The third segment occurs in the morning and concerns the survivors who have returned to their vacation home. Central to the novel is the Ramseys' marriage, and Mrs. Ramsey's power as an artist and creator gives the story a mystical charm.

In *To the Lighthouse*, Woolf further refined and built on the writing devices she introduced in *Jacob's Room* and *Mrs. Dalloway*. She relied on characterization, rather than plot, to advance the story, and, as she often did, she established *creation* as an underlying theme. One of her characters, for example, is a painter who observes the inevitable drifting apart of the family members. Through this character, Woolf describes both the difficulty and the beauty of the creative process, the process of expressing the self:

> . . . [S]he took her hand and raised her brush. For a moment it stayed trembling in a painful but exciting ecstasy in the air. Where to begin? . . . One line placed on the canvas committed her to innumerable risks, to frequent and irrevocable decisions. . . . Still the risk must be run; the mark made.

... The brush descended. It flickered brown over the white canvas; it left a running mark. A second time she did it—a third time. And so pausing and so flickering, she attained a dancing rhythmical movement, as if the pauses were one part of the rhythm and the strokes

WOOLF AGAINST REALISM IN FILM

In "The Cinema" (1926), Woolf turns her thoughts toward the relationship between literature and the emerging art of film. Before the early 1930s, the cinema—like novels and short stories before World War I—had been used mainly to tell stories in a "realistic" way, showing events to the viewer in the order in which those events took place. In this essay, Woolf argues against this. She advocates the kind of story-telling that she, James Joyce, T.S. Eliot, and other Modernists were working to bring about in literature since the end of the war: not linear, plot-based realism, but a more accurate depiction of the fragmentary psychology, emotions, and perceptions of human life. These ideas would catch on in film within a few years of Woolf's writing—especially in France, where in the 1930s directors such as Jean Renoir, Luis Buñuel (who collaborated with the master Surrealist Salvador Dalí), and Jean Cocteau replaced storytelling with strong, disjunct, and often repellent images. In this passage, Woolf invokes Anna Karenina, a character from the Russian master novelist Leo Tolstoy, to illustrate the shortcomings of cinematic realism:

All the famous novels of the world, with their well-known characters, and their famous scenes, only asked, it seemed, to be put on the films. . . . The cinema fell another, and all were related; and so, lightly and swiftly pausing, striking, she scored her canvas with brown running nervous lines which had no sooner settled there than they enclosed (she felt it looming out at her) a space. . . . [W]hat could be more formidable than that

upon its prey with immense rapacity, and to this moment largely subsists upon the body of its unfortunate victim. But the results are disastrous to both. The alliance is unnatural. Eye and brain are torn asunder ruthlessly as they try vainly to work in couples. The eye says: 'Here is Anna Karenina.' A voluptuous lady in black velvet wearing pearls comes before us. But the brain says: 'That is no more Anna Karenina than it is Queen Victoria.' For the brain knows Anna almost entirely by the inside of her mind—her charm, her passion, her despair. All the emphasis is laid by the cinema upon her teeth, her pearls, and her velvet. Then 'Anna falls in love with Vronsky'—that is to say, the lady in black velvet falls into the arms of a gentleman in uniform, and they kiss with enormous succulence, great deliberation, and infinite gesticulation on a sofa in an extremely well-appointed library, while a gardener incidentally mows the lawn. So we lurch and lumber through the most famous novels of the world. So we spell them out in words of one syllable written, too, in the scrawl of an illiterate schoolboy. A kiss is love. A broken cup is jealousy. A grin is happiness. Death is a hearse. None of these things has the least connection with the novel that Tolstoy wrote. . . .

space? . . . [S]he heard some voice saying she couldn't paint, saying she couldn't create. . . .

. . . Then . . . she began precariously dipping among the blues and umbers, moving her brush hither and thither, but it was now heavier and went slower, as if it had fallen in with some rhythm which was dictated to her. . . . And as she lost consciousness of outer things, and her name and her personality and her appearance . . . her mind kept throwing up from its depths scenes, and names, and sayings, and memories and ideas, like a fountain spurting over that glaring, hideously difficult white space, while she modelled it with greens and blues.

Once again, Woolf employed stream of consciousness to drive the narration and capture the essence of the novel's characters—particularly that of Mrs. Ramsey. And she devoted an entire section of the book to depicting the passage of time and the *absence* of characters:

. . . [W]ith the house empty and the doors locked and the mattresses rolled round, those stray airs, advance guards of great armies, blustered in, brushed bare boards, nibbled and fanned, met nothing in bedroom or drawing-room that wholly resisted them but only hangings that flapped, wood that creaked, the bare legs of tables, saucepans and china already furred, tarnished, cracked. What people had shed and left—a pair of shoes, a shooting cap, some faded skirts and coats in wardrobes—those alone kept the human shape and in the emptiness indicated how once they were filled and animated; how once hands were busy with hooks and buttons; how once the looking-glass had held a face; had held a world hollowed out in which a figure turned, a hand flashed, the door opened, in came children rushing and tumbling; and went out again. Now, day after day, light turned, like a flower reflected in water, its sharp image on the wall opposite. Only the shadows of the trees, flourishing in the wind, made obeisance on the wall, and for a moment darkened the pool in which light reflected itself; or birds, flying, made a soft spot flutter slowly across the bedroom floor.

She carefully positioned bits of straight narrative into these passages—enclosing each piece of narration in brackets. By weaving the symbol of the lighthouse and the inherent beauty of nature into the story, Woolf gave the story the poetic depth and vision that caused it to become a favorite among her readers. The poet and critic Edwin Muir wrote, "For imagination and beauty of writing, it is probably not surpassed in contemporary prose." (Nicolson, 103) The finesse with which Woolf had written the novel, specifically the chapter entitled "Time Passes" (from which the above passage was taken), impressed her readers and won her the Femina Prize, one of England's most prestigious literary awards.

ORLANDO

By the time *To the Lighthouse* was published in 1927, Woolf's anxiety had risen, as it always seemed to in the final stages of a manuscript's revision. To ease her stress, Woolf set aside her innovative fiction to focus on some lighter writing projects. She wrote, "I feel the need of an escapade after these serious poetic experimental books whose form is always so closely considered. I want to kick up my heels and be off." (Lehmann, 60) The first of the two projects she chose to work on was a novel called *Orlando*, inspired by her friend Vita Sackville-West.

Woolf met Sackville-West in December of 1922 at a party hosted by Clive Bell. In spite of her initial impressions of Vita, whom she considered to be "parakeet colored, with all the supple ease of the aristocracy, but not the wit of an artist,"

Woolf found Vita attractive, and the two became friends. (Nicolson, 84) Vita was dark-eyed, beautiful, and majestic, and was descended from an aristocratic family. She lacked the quick wit required to fit into the Bloomsbury Group; but she shared Woolf's interest in literature and writing, and her literary reputation at the time rivaled Woolf's. Over time, they developed a passionate love for each other and became almost inseparable. In a diary entry dated December 21, 1925, Woolf describes Vita as a Sapphist—a kind of shorthand for a woman with homosexual tendencies, derived from the Greek poet Sappho, whose poetry is often cited in a lesbian context:

> These Sapphists love women; friendship is never untinged with amorosity. In short, my fears and refrainings, my 'impertinence,' my usual self-consciousness in intercourse with people who mayn't want me and so on—were all, as L. said, sheer fudge; and partly thanks to him (he made me write) I wound up this wounded and stricken year in great style. I like her and being with her and the splendour—she shines in the grocer's shop in Sevenoaks with a candle lit radiance, stalking on legs like beech trees, pink glowing, grape clustered, pearl hung. That is the secret of her glamour, I suppose. Anyhow she found me incredibly dowdy. No woman cared less for personal appearance. No one put on things in the way I did. Yet so beautiful, etc.

Moreover, she seems to envy her friend for being "a real woman" and a maternal figure, but she also appears to doubt the reality of her admiration:

> What is the effect of all this on me? Very mixed. There is her maturity and full breastedness; her being so much in full sail on the high tides, where I am coasting down backwaters; her capacity I mean to take the floor in any

company, to represent her country, to visit Chatsworth to control silver, servants, chow dogs; her motherhood (but she is a little cold and off-hand with her boys); her being in short (what I have never been) a real woman. Then there is some voluptuousness about her; the grapes are ripe; and not reflective. No. In brain and insight she is not as highly organised as I am. But then she is aware of this and so lavishes on me the maternal protection which, for some reason, is what I have always most wished from everyone. What L. gives me, and Nessa gives me and Vita, in her more clumsy external way, tries to give me. For of course, mingled with all this glamour, grape clusters and pearl necklaces, there is something loose fitting. How much, for example, shall I really miss her when she is motoring across the desert? (Woolf, *A Writer's Diary*)

Her friendship with Vita became intense. Using Vita as a model for her main character, Woolf began her novel *Orlando* in the autumn of 1927. *Orlando* is a complicated and dazzling novel, a fantastic voyage through English history and literature. Woolf based the character of Orlando wholly on Vita, and as a joke, she included several illustrations in the book that portrayed Vita as Orlando. The narrator is a biographer, and the title character begins the novel as a sixteen-year-old boy in the sixteenth century and ends the novel at the stroke of midnight on October 11, 1928—the book's date of publication—as a thirty-six-year-old woman. Over the course of the story, Orlando meets many famous people, including Queen Elizabeth I, Alexander Pope, and William Shakespeare, and travels to many places, such as England and Turkey. The novel defies conventions of time, space, and gender.

From start to finish, Woolf wrote *Orlando* as a humorous work, filled with whimsical images and unlikely situations. Woolf said that she wanted it to be "half laughing, half serious, with great splashes of exaggeration," and in that,

Orlando fulfilled her intentions. (Lehmann, 63) She understood that *Orlando* was not as innovative as her more serious fiction, but Woolf used the fantasy to explore literature and cross social barriers. She characterized each period through which Orlando traveled, describing the Victorian era for example, as a dark, menacing cloud. Orlando's sex change enabled Woolf to universalize her title character and challenge traditional gender expectations.

Woolf found that writing *Orlando* was therapeutic, and with it, she continued her pattern of crafting innovative novels followed by easy-to-read "holiday" books. For instance, *The Voyage Out* was demanding, while she enjoyed her work on *Night and Day*; *To the Lighthouse* was a struggle, while *Orlando* was a joy to write. Through her illness, Woolf had examined her personal limits. She realized that she had to balance her sanity with her creativity. As a result, she developed a writing cycle in which unique novels that endangered her mental stability were followed by playful, more conservative books that enabled her to recuperate.

Not until *Orlando* was published were the Woolfs financially secure. Its lighthearted style boosted Woolf's popularity and made her a commercial success. While *To the Lighthouse* sold 3,873 copies in its first year, *Orlando* sold 8,104 copies in its first six months. She wrote in her diary:

> For the first time since I married, 1912–1928—16 years, I have been spending money. The spending muscle does not work naturally yet. I feel guilty; put off buying, when I know that I should buy; and yet have an agreeable luxurious sense of coins in my pocket beyond my weekly 13/—which was always running out, or being encroached upon. (Lehmann, 69)

She earned about £3,020 in 1929, and in February of 1930 she noted that *A Room of One's Own* sold 10,000 copies,

Vita Sackville-West. In 1923, Clive Bell introduced Virginia Woolf to Vita Sackville-West, an aristocratic but progressive poet and novelist. Many critics speculate that the two soon fell in love and began a passionate affair, but the extent of their attraction is difficult to determine. Woolf drew on Sackville-West's personality to create the androgynous protagonist in her novel *Orlando*. This photograph was taken in 1916 by one of the primary British Modernist photographers, E.O. Hoppé, who within a decade would become one of the best-known photographers in the world.

promising additional financial security. Readers acknowledged that her work was difficult to read and experimental, but many anticipated its impact on fiction. With *Orlando*, Woolf became the fashionable author for socialites to read, and her following grew as more readers joined her groundbreaking literary movement.

SPEAKING HER MIND

Woolf balanced the ups and downs of writing fiction with her nonfiction works. She continued to write reviews, biographies, and essays throughout her life. These provided some relief from the demands her fiction made on her imagination, and they offered the Woolfs a steady source of income. She wrote her best-known nonfiction piece, a polemic she called *A Room of One's Own*, in the fall of 1928.

Written from her lecture notes, *A Room of One's Own* called for female emancipation (economic and otherwise), a rejection of complacency in all forms, and a challenge for each generation to strengthen the freedom of women. To illustrate the differences between a man's education and a woman's informal schooling, she contrasted the established university system of Oxford and Cambridge (or, as many referred to it, "Oxbridge"), with its exclusive library and gourmet meals, with Girton College, a women's college that served a meager evening supper. Through the essay, Woolf explored the "ancient and obscure emotions" that caused fathers throughout history to control and limit their daughters. She established the connections between a male-dominated world, a warlike world, and a world devoted to making money. Women, she argued, must "think back through our mothers" and assert their need for education, professional training, and a public life. To make her point, Woolf imagined that Shakespeare had an equally brilliant sister who, like her brother, wanted to be a poet. Due to societal constraints, however, she became pregnant with the child of a theater manager and committed suicide, ensuring that not a word of what she wrote would survive:

> I told you in the course of this paper that Shakespeare had a sister; but do not look for her in Sir Sidney Lee's life of the poet. She died young—alas, she never wrote a word. She lies buried where the omnibuses now stop, opposite the Elephant and Castle. Now my belief is that this poet who never wrote a word and was buried at the crossroads still lives. She lives in you and in me, and in many other women who are not here tonight, for they are washing up the dishes and putting the children to bed. But she lives; for great poets do not die; they are continuing presences; they need only the opportunity to walk among us in the flesh . . . For my belief is that if we live another century or so . . . if we have the habit of freedom and the courage to write exactly what we think . . . then the opportunity will come and the dead poet who was Shakespeare's sister will put on the body which she has so often laid down. (*A Room of One's Own*, 124–125)

Despite the wit and humor with which it was written, *A Room of One's Own* created a hailstorm of controversy. Its frank criticism of societal norms and its overt feminist arguments shocked men and women alike. Many readers were uncomfortable with Woolf's views on women's liberation, although over time, *A Room of One's Own* became a mainstay of the feminist movement.

With a growing reputation and increased book sales, Woolf's income began to afford her luxuries. She and Leonard made small improvements to Monk's House. They bought a gramophone, and in the summer of 1927, purchased a car. Despite driving lessons, Woolf lost control of the car during one of her early excursions and drove it through a hedge. Leaving the driving to Leonard, the Woolfs explored the countryside, from castles to seashores. She wrote, "I like driving off to Rodmell on a hot Friday evening and having cold ham, and sitting on my terrace and smoking a cigar with an owl or two." The Woolfs drove through western and southern Europe, stopping to visit Vanessa, Duncan Grant, and the Bell children, who spent much of the year in southern France. Woolf enjoyed her time away from London, and she delighted in the sights and sounds of her journeys.

Her life settled into gentler rhythms for a time, and Woolf enjoyed her quiet life with Leonard and her dog Pinker. Pinker was one of many dogs Woolf had throughout her life. She was fascinated by animals, and loved to try to imagine what they were feeling. She imagined that she took on a certain animal's personality in different relationships: With Vanessa she saw herself as a goat, following along; with Leonard she was a mandrill, mated and potentially ferocious; with Vita she was a cocker spaniel, wanting to please. She even wrote a story called "Flush" in which the main character is a dog stolen from poet Elizabeth Barrett Browning.

To ease her tensions, the Woolfs enforced a structured routine that supported Virginia's blooming creativity. Her diary provided her daily schedule:

> I get up at half past eight and walk across the garden. . . . I wash and go in to breakfast which is laid on the check tablecloth. With luck I may have an interesting letter; today there was none. And then bath and dress; and come out here and write or correct for three hours, broken at 11 by Leonard with milk and perhaps newspapers. At one, luncheon—rissoles today and chocolate custard. A brief reading and smoking after lunch; and at about two I change into thick shoes, take Pinker's [her dog's] lead and go out—up to Asheham hill this afternoon, where I sat a minute or two, and then home again along the river. Tea at four, about; and then I come out here and write several

letters. . . . And soon the bell will ring and we shall dine
and then we shall have some music and I shall smoke a
cigar; and then we shall read . . . and so to bed. Now my
little tugging and distressing book and articles are off
my mind my brain seems to fill and expand and grow
physically light and peaceful. . . . And so the unconscious
part now expands; and walking I notice the red corn and
blue of the plain and an infinite number of things without
naming them. (Q. Bell, 2.148)

Her creative efforts extended through bedtime, where
everyday people and events mixed in her subconscious to
become her art. Woolf's sleep came quickly many nights in the
country, because the walks she took were often six to seven
miles long. She would leap over fences, barbed wire, and
ditches. These were precious and productive days, but they
were numbered.

THE WAVES

Between 1927 and 1931, Woolf created her next masterpiece.
Originally titled "The Moths," *The Waves* tells the story of six
friends, three male and three female. The setting of the novel is
unclear and unimportant, as the text traces the lives of the
six characters in nine episodes. Separating each episode is a
symbolic interlude that marks the passing of time through the
images of the sun and the sea. In each episode, the characters'
soliloquies reveal their levels of maturity, from childhood
to middle age, with some episodes focusing on characters'
fantasies and dreams and others depicting life-altering events
that the characters experience. The growth of each character is
highlighted by the two social gatherings that the friends
attend—a farewell dinner and a reunion at Hampton Court.
But the characters' differences emphasize their similarities, as
one character's final soliloquy suggests: "It is not one life that I
look back upon; I am not one person; I am many people . . . nor

Vanessa Bell, 1942. This portrait of Vanessa was painted in 1942 by Duncan Grant, with whom Vanessa had been romantically involved as early as 1924. Vanessa, about 57 years old at the time of this portrait, had become a fashionable painter like Grant. She appears here approximately one year after Virginia's death.

do I always know if I am man or woman, Bernard or Neville, Louis, Susan, Jinny or Rhonda." (Lehmann, 84) Woolf suggests that interactions link people together in such a way that "we are the same person, and not separate people." (Nicolson, 117)

From beginning to end, *The Waves* was a challenge for Woolf to write. In September of 1929, she recorded in her diary, "I write two pages of arrant nonsense, after straining; I write variations of every sentence; compromises; bad shots; possibilities; till my writing book is like a lunatic's dream." (Lehmann, 77) Her headaches resumed as she revised the second version of the novel, and hallucinations and exhaustion kept her bed-ridden for six weeks. When she recovered sufficiently, she continued to write, working steadily through 1930 and finishing the manuscript on February 7, 1931. Her relief upon completing *The Waves* was immense, and she recorded her joy:

> I must record, heaven be praised, the end of *The Waves*. I wrote the words O Death fifteen minutes ago, having reeled across the last ten pages with some moments of such intensity and intoxication that I seemed only to stumble after my own voice, or almost, after some sort of speaker (as when I was mad). . . . Whether good or bad, it's done; and, as I certainly felt at the end, not merely finished, but rounded off, completed. . . . I have netted that fin in the waste of water which appeared to me over the marshes out of my window . . . when I was coming to an end of *To the Lighthouse*. (Q. Bell, 2.157)

The Waves represents Woolf's most innovative and most polished novel. In it, she strips away detail and narrative analysis to illustrate the essence of life from youth to maturity. The pace of the prose is slower than that of *To the Lighthouse* and *Mrs. Dalloway*, but the background image of the waves in the sea lends subtle movement to the novel. She integrates prose, poetry, and a play to create a lyrical work that she claimed was the only one of her books she could read with pleasure.

The Waves, like several of Woolf's earlier works, attempts to represent the passing of time—significant interludes between events in the story. In *The Saturday Review of Literature*, an American university professor praised Woolf's experimentation with time, as well as her characteristic Modernist experimentation with form:

> [S]he has come nearer to fusing prose and poetry into an expression of unapproached beauty than she has in any of her previous writing. . . . Mrs Woolf has experimented with time passing in *To the Lighthouse* and in *Orlando*. In *The Waves* she passes beyond experiment to mature accomplishment, so that I venture the verdict that better than any other novelist she has solved one of the major problems of fiction, and has actually given the reader a full realization of the time element. . . . Time and change, the impinging of time and experience upon individuals make up the important substance of *The Waves*. . . . *The Waves* is a novel of first importance; one of the few which have come in our own day with so much as a small chance to survive the vigorous test of time. (Majumdar)

Harold Nicolson, a friend of the Woolfs who later married Vita Sackville-West, was even more complimentary in *Action*:

> Her whole intention is to depict the fluidity of human experience, the insistent interest of the inconsequent, the half-realised, the half-articulate, the unfinished and the unfinishable. . . . Her aim is to convey the half-lights of human experience and the fluid edges of personal identity. Her six characters fuse, towards the end, into a synthesis of sensation. It is important that this book should be read twice over. The book is difficult. Yet it is superb. (Majumdar)

Other reviewers were less inclined to accept Woolf's experimentation; their criticisms seem to have been based mainly on the book's emphasis on style rather than substance. An example appeared in *The San Francisco Chronicle* in December of 1931:

> Most people are going to find *The Waves* extremely difficult reading—all people, in fact, excepting those who are prepared to accept the author's highly artificial trick in writing it for the sake of the poetic images she invokes. . . . [The characters] are simply six Mrs Woolfs, they are not more than attenuated shadows—brilliant, many-sided, tricky, but still shadows—of the real people the reader has a right to expect. . . . No doubt it is a beautiful exercise, but it lacks the reality, the passion, the association with life that would bring it into relation with those who must read it. And lacking that passion, that association, it lacks the significance that would make it a fine book. (Majumdar)

On the whole, the critical reviews were very favorable, and the book was a commercial success as well; 6,500 copies were sold in three weeks. Critical esteem for the novel has only grown in the seventy years since its publication, and now most critics consider *The Waves* Woolf's finest literary achievement.

8

A Battlefield of Emotions

1931–1941

It's not catastrophes, murders, deaths, diseases, that age and kill us;
it's the way people look and laugh, and run up the steps of omnibuses.
— Virginia Woolf, *Jacob's Room* (1922)

Following the publication of *The Waves*, the Woolfs decided to resume their travels. They took two trips, one wonderful and one ominous. In April of 1932, Woolf toured Greece with Leonard, Roger Fry, and Fry's sister Margery. They got off to an amusing start when they accidentally purchased two black goats and a bowl of sour milk as they asked for directions. Woolf was fascinated by the countryside and wrote: "How lovely the pure lip of the sea touching a wild shore, with hills behind, and green plains and red rocks." She noted that "pure sea water on pure sand is almost the loveliest thing in the world." She was equally interested in

Virginia Woolf, 1932. This haunting photograph, also by E.O. Hoppé, was taken when most of Woolf's major works had already been published. Toward the end of her life, Woolf began to lose confidence in her writing. Although her works remained popular in the literary movements of the day, events in her personal life and her own fears led to her growing dissatisfaction with her work. Nevertheless, she continued writing until the day of her death.

the people she met: "We saw the Greek shepherds' hut in a wood near Marathon, and a lovely dark-olive, red-lipped, pink-shawled girl wandering and spinning thread from a lump of wool." With Fry, Woolf traveled with a world expert on classical art, but she seemed less fascinated by the temples and churches. She enjoyed her stay in Greece tremendously and said that she "could love Greece as an old woman as [she] once loved Cornwall as a child." (Nicolson, 124–125)

In the spring of 1935 Leonard and Woolf traveled to Europe again, this time to Holland, Germany, Austria, and Italy. It was a dangerous time to travel. Leonard, who was Jewish, had been warned by the foreign office to avoid Germany. Indeed, they found anti-Semitic propaganda posted around every German town they visited. When they went to Bonn, one of Adolf Hitler's main officers, Hermann Göring, was also there for a rally. Security was tight, and Hitler's storm troopers surrounded their car at one point. Fortunately, Leonard's pet marmoset, Mitz, amused and distracted the guards, who allowed the Woolfs through the barriers. It was a close call, as Leonard almost certainly would not have backed down from a confrontation (he usually welcomed them).

By this time, Woolf's books had enjoyed much success in America. She never crossed the Atlantic and she never visited America, although she received several invitations. Instead, she imagined America as a wonderland and as a nightmare. She considered the American Midwest "unattractive and, largely sprinkled with old tin kettles—racing across vast slabs of plate glass." On the other hand, she romanticized Hollywood as "a marble city gleaming at your feet; and people so new, so brave, so beautiful and utterly uncontaminated by civilization, popping in and out of booths and theaters with pistols in their hands and aeroplanes soaring over their heads." New York merely housed her American publisher, Harcourt Brace. She maintained correspondence with several American friends, whom she generally considered to be British unless they irritated her. (Nicolson, 126–127)

Woolf and Leonard traveled more in the 1930s because the

money from her writing afforded their travel. In addition, they had more time to travel because they no longer saw their Bloomsbury friends frequently. Their friends had become so successful that demands on their time were extraordinary. Keynes was a senior economist and his valuable opinions were very much in demand. MacCarthy was the leading literary critic of the day, and Strachey was writing a string of best-sellers. Eliot had become a professor at Harvard, and Fry was a professor at Cambridge. Duncan Grant and Vanessa were fashionable painters. Their busy schedules made it a challenge to get together, but they still enjoyed one another's company and often shared stories of their adventures.

THE WORLD CHANGES

The attitudes of the Bloomsbury Group had not changed, but the world had. Women could vote and enter the professions; both sex before marriage and homosexual love were tolerated, though not actually embraced; pacifist views were on the rise again after the devastation of World War I and the establishment of the League of Nations. The unconventional beliefs of the Bloomsbury friends had become conventional. However, the troubling rise of Adolf Hitler's Third Reich and other fascist regimes weakened the Bloomsbury Group's pacifism; moreover, it caused the group's focus on the arts to seem like an expensive luxury. It was hard for people to value the arts, literature, and abstract political theory when German air raids threatened to destroy Europe. The world was becoming fractured, and the Bloomsbury Group felt the impending changes sooner than most.

The first of the fractures in Bloomsbury was Lytton Strachey's death in 1932 from stomach cancer. Woolf had always admired Strachey's wit, and she had considered him one of her dearest friends. She wrote, "He is the most sympathetic and understanding friend to talk to. . . . If one adds his peculiar flavour of mind, his wit and infinite intelligence, he is a figure not to be replaced." (Nicolson, 61) They were kindred spirits, who shared jokes and exchanged criticism of each other's works. Upon his death, she wrote to their mutual friend Lady Ottoline, "I have got a queer feeling that I'm hearing him talk in the next room—the talk I always want to go on with. I have a million things to tell him, and never shall." (Nicolson, 129) Woolf would miss him.

In 1934, the Bloomsbury Group suffered another blow with the sudden death of Roger Fry. He had been the life of the Bloomsbury parties and a close friend since he joined their circle in 1910. He had once attended an *Alice in Wonderland* party given by Vanessa dressed as the White Knight. He had attached candles, mousetraps, frying pans, and other objects to his outfit as children gathered around and squealed with delight. Woolf missed Fry horribly—at times even more than she missed Strachey—and she resolved to write his biography, which finally went to press in 1940. Fry's death further weakened Woolf's already unstable mental health.

Woolf felt her world fracture even further when the land near her country home, Monk's House, was degraded. A cement company moved in and built vast corrugated iron sheds, polluting the whole valley with a fine white dust. Many trees died, while dog-racing tracks and new developments moved in. Woolf observed this "progress" with despair.

WRITING THROUGH *THE YEARS*

While writing "Flush," Woolf began to outline a new novel. She envisioned it as a new form of fiction, a factual novel. In her diary, she wrote, "It's to be an Essay-Novel called *The Pargiters*—and it's to take in everything, sex, education, life, etc.: and come, with the most powerful and agile leaps, like a chamois, across the precipices from 1880 to here and now." (Lehmann, 95) She intended *The Pargiters*, later renamed *The Years*, to serve as a semi-fictional extension of *A Room of One's Own*. Her initial draft consisted of six essays interspersed with fictional illustrations. It also included her ideas about transforming reality into fiction.

Unhappy with the novel's progress, she attempted to collapse the essay into the main text three months later. Still, the novel failed to meet her expectations. She began to experience unusual difficulty with her writing, which she

WOOLF ON KNOWING ONE'S AUDIENCE

From "The Patron and the Crocus" (1925):

Young men and women beginning to write are generally given the plausible but utterly impracticable advice to write what they have to write as shortly as possible, as clearly as possible, and without other thought in their minds except to say exactly what is in them. Nobody ever adds on these occasions the one thing needful: "And be sure you choose your patron wisely," though that is the gist of the whole matter. For a book is always written for somebody to read, and, since the patron is not merely the paymaster, but also in a very subtle and insidious way the instigator and inspirer of what is written, it is of the utmost importance that he should be a desirable man.

. . . Thus the writer who has been moved by the sight of the first crocus in Kensington Gardens has, before he sets pen to paper, to choose from a crowd of competitors the particular patron who suits him best. It is futile to say, "Dismiss them all; think only of your crocus," because writing is a method of communication; and the crocus is an imperfect crocus until it has been shared. The first man or the last may write for himself alone, but he is an exception and an unenviable one at that, and the gulls are welcome to his works if the gulls can read them.

described as a persistent cough, with fact and fiction colliding to form a strained story. She wrote sixty thousand words of the novel, only to throw them away and start over. With each revision, Woolf's mental stability weakened. She continued to struggle with her writing. She noted, "I have never suffered, since *The Voyage Out*, such acute despair on re-reading, as this time." (Leaska, 373) *The Years* became so personal that she worried that the book's possible failure reflected a failure of her life, and she sank further into her depression. Finally, after four years of painful revisions, she finished the book that was featured on the cover of *Time*. *The Years* was published in March of 1937.

The Years tells the story of a family during a fifty-year period. It is largely autobiographical, with the characters demonstrating many traits of her family members, the Bloomsbury Group, and Woolf herself. The novel focuses on a young woman's growing determination and shows how experience can be both beneficial and harmful. It is much harsher than her previous works, emphasizing society's cruelty due to class, race, and gender.

Despite Woolf's fears and insecurities, *The Years* became an immediate success. Critics praised the novel, and it was a best-seller on both sides of the Atlantic. In America, *The Years* sold 25,000 copies within two months, restoring Woolf's diminished bank account. Its reception validated Woolf for a time, but slowly her despair returned.

Woolf seems to have lost her desire to experiment with the novel as a literary form, and she was viewed more and more as part of the literary establishment, no longer considered the visionary and groundbreaker she once had been. The revolution in literature for which she, T.S. Eliot, D.H. Lawrence, James Joyce, E.M. Forster, William Faulkner, and others were responsible had been won, but in the process of fighting it had lost its power. By the mid-1930s, Lawrence was dead, Joyce hadn't written anything in ten years, and Forster had stopped writing altogether. In *The Years*, Woolf seemed to lose her own creative edge. She had always felt that she was "a battlefield of emotions," but this feeling became common, as the world became the setting for World War II.

With the rise of Hitler and the Great Depression, the young writers of the time called for literature that dealt with different themes and led to political action. These new writers wanted to write about war and class struggles, and Woolf was no longer near the center of the literary world. She was by instinct a pacifist, and she had difficulty believing that the best response to anger and war was more anger and more war. She could not see how fighting evil with evil could lead to a better world. She also felt that wars brought benefits to an elite few, and those benefits were never shared widely. To denounce war in all its forms, she wrote an essay called "Three Guineas" that was as angry as anything she had ever written. She felt she was living in a very dangerous time, and that the danger came from an instinctive aggression in men that had not been changed by civilization.

Similar to *A Room of One's Own*, "Three Guineas" is a polemic that provides a strong argument against male privileges and institutions and condemns war. "Three Guineas", however, lacks the lightness and humor of *A Room of One's Own*. Instead, it reflects Woolf's anguish at the death of her favorite nephew, Julian Bell, during the Spanish Civil War. In it, she angrily blames men for war and highlights the need for women's involvement in politics, inferring that with women's input, war would not exist. It is a claim for pacifism, what she referred to as her "war pamphlet." (Nicolson, 159) "Three Guineas" was published to positive, but not shining, reviews. Ironically, Woolf's female critics expressed the harshest criticism.

As the beginning of World War II neared, Woolf felt a deep conflict between her pacifism and her support for Leonard. His political career and influence had continued to grow—he had almost become a member of Parliament. He

Leonard Woolf. Virginia's sister, Vanessa, painted this portrait of Leonard at his desk in 1940, when he and Virginia had been married for about twenty-eight years. As Virginia's fame had grown, so had Leonard's. His own literary success led him to prestigious assignments in his field. The Woolfs took great pride in each other's works and achievements. This mutual respect and admiration held their relationship together for almost thirty years, through otherwise trying times.

felt England needed to unite with the Soviet Union to fight Germany in a war he saw as inevitable. Woolf thought Hitler "a ridiculous little man," and she did not support war as the only option. (Nicolson, 168) To her, war meant chaos, and no one but the worst people thrived in true chaos. She remembered the air raids of World War I, and understood the consequences of military action. She feared that she would not live another year. She was not far wrong.

On September 3, 1939, Britain and France declared war on Germany. The Woolfs left for Monk's House upon hearing the news to avoid being trapped in London. Woolf felt a "dumb rage" at being "fought for by young people whom one wants to see making love." (Nicolson, 176) To hide their lights and protect their lives, the Woolfs and their neighbors blackened the windows of their houses. The winter of 1939–1940 was the coldest on record, and Woolf and Leonard suffered through it with deepening pessimism and despair. They debated what to do if the Nazis invaded, which they expected at any time. With Monk's House in the path of any land invasion to London, they began to prepare for the worst. They resolved that if they ever saw Nazis approaching the house, they would lock themselves in the garage and commit suicide either with morphine provided by Adrian Stephen or with lethal car fumes, for which purpose they kept gasoline on hand. They were constantly on the alert, looking over their shoulders and listening for the menacing sounds of an advancing army.

In August and September of 1940, the Battle of Britain was fought in the sky overhead. Woolf wrote:

> They [the German planes] came very close. We lay down under the tree. The sound was like someone sawing in the air just above us. We lay flat on our faces, hands behind head. Don't close your teeth, said L. . . . Bombs shook the windows of my lodge. Will it drop I asked? If so, we shall be broken together. (Q. Bell, 2.217)

Despite her pacifism, Woolf hated the swastikas she saw painted on the German planes as they flew over. When she watched a squadron of British fighter planes, she "instinctively wished them luck." She admired Prime Minister Winston Churchill and his "clear, measured, robust" speeches. She even began to admire the politicians who had a "grim good sense" about the war effort. Leonard and her friends admired her courage, as Woolf refused to live in fear. (Nicolson, 179)

Woolf regretted her resolution to write about Roger Fry's life almost immediately after starting his biography in 1938. In her diary, she referred to it as a "grind," and her references to it were rarely happy. She worried about capturing the details of his life, including his wife's insanity (she was institutionalized) and his short-term love affair with Vanessa. While Vanessa didn't mind Woolf's revealing the true nature of her affair with Fry, Woolf was uncomfortable with making her sister's affair so public. As a compromise, she referred to their relationship as a "friendship." When she finally completed the biography, Woolf allowed Leonard, Vanessa, and Margery Fry, Roger's sister, to read the manuscript. Leonard disliked it; Vanessa found it deeply moving; and Margery loved it, writing, "It's *him.*" *Roger Fry: A Biography* was published in July of 1940 and sold well. Unfortunately, the sales did nothing to reassure Woolf's dwindling confidence in her writing. (Lehmann, 104)

While completing Fry's biography, Woolf worked on what was to be her final novel, *Between the Acts.* This novel, set in the English countryside, focused on "the struggle of civilization against savagery; of what is spiritually inspiring against squalor and greed; of love against lust, against what is destructive and selfish in sexual appetite." The action occurs in a single day at one location, with the fates of the characters intertwined by their desires and their dislikes.

Between the Acts is a complex book in which the rise and fall of civilizations is echoed through much of the story. Woolf died before completing her final revisions, and critics expressed

Portrait of Virginia. This portrait, created when Woolf was twenty-four years old, captures her bold and defiant spirit. She was always a bit of a rabble-rouser in her day, speaking on issues that no one else would approach and working with styles of writing that didn't always meet with critical approval. Her strong and rebellious nature gave birth to some of the most progressive and boundary-breaking literature of the early twentieth century. This portrait was sketched by Francis Dodd, one of Britain's leading portrait artists, in 1908.

mixed feelings about it. Several considered it too fragmented, but Leonard and others found it "more vigorous and pulled together than most of her other books, to have more depth and to be very moving." The latter opinion has gained acceptance, and recent critics consider it a masterpiece, albeit in rougher form than her other novels. (Lehmann, 106–108)

As usual, her revisions to *Between the Acts* led to headaches and depression. Despite Leonard's attempts to prevent another episode of insanity, her condition was so weakened after *The Years* that a relapse was nearly inevitable. Symptoms of Woolf's mental instability reappeared in earnest in January of 1941. At that time, World War II was felt everywhere, and people were preparing for a land invasion of England. The Woolf home in London had been destroyed during air raids in 1940. Food was rationed, and travel was impossible. These incidents provided more fuel for her illness. By March of the same year, she had become convinced that she could not withstand another onslaught from the voices in her head; her world was coming to an end.

On March 28, 1941, Woolf wrote farewell letters to Vanessa and Leonard. Following a plan she had devised in case of such a mental crisis, she walked to the River Ouse, which was swollen by spring rains, and weighted herself with large stones that she put in the pocket of her fur coat. Virginia Woolf then drowned herself in the river.

Leonard found her suicide letter:

> Dearest, I feel certain that I am going mad again. I feel we can't go though another of those terrible times. . . . So I am doing what seems the best thing to do. You have given me the greatest happiness possible. You have been in every way all that anyone could be. . . . Everything has gone from me but the certainty of your goodness. I don't think two people could have been happier than we have been. (Q. Bell, 2.226)

Her life had ended, but her influence on the world had just begun. Her novels and essays became treasures of English literature. Her love of ideas, books, people, and reading live untouched. Woolf was not religious, but she evokes an image of an afterlife in her essay "How Should One Read a Book?" In this essay, which appeared in her *Second Common Reader*, she describes her passion for reading, a passion that she has handed down to her readers:

> I have sometimes dreamt, at least, that when the Day of Judgment dawns and the great conquerors and lawyers and statesman come to receive their rewards—their crowns, their laurels, their names carved indelibly upon imperishable marble—the Almighty will turn to Peter and will say, not without a certain envy when He sees us coming with our books under our arms, 'Look, these need no reward. We have nothing to give them here. They have loved reading.'

1868   Birth of George Duckworth.

1869   Birth of Stella Duckworth.

1870   Birth of Gerald Duckworth; birth of Laura Stephen.

1876   Birth of Vanessa Stephen.

1880   Birth of Julian Thoby Stephen.

1882   Born Adeline Virginia Stephen on January 25, at 22 Hyde Park Gate, London, England.

1883   Birth of Adrian Stephen.

1895   Mother, Julia Stephen, dies; first episode of Woolf's mental illness; Stella Duckworth assumes the household responsibilities.

1897   Begins her first diary; marriage and death of Stella Duckworth.

1904   Father, Sir Leslie Stephen, dies; second major episode of mental illness and first suicide attempt; Woolf publishes first essays, some unsigned; Leonard Woolf appears at a Bloomsbury gathering on November 17.

1905   Brother Thoby invites friends for parties/discussions; Bloomsbury Group is created.

1906   Brother Thoby dies from typhoid fever caught in Greece.

1907   Sister Vanessa marries Clive Bell; Woolf shares an apartment with Adrian.

1910   *Dreadnought* Hoax; Roger Fry organizes First Post-Impressionist Exhibition.

1912   Marries Leonard Woolf.

1913   *The Voyage Out* is accepted for publication; third and possibly worst major episode of Woolf's mental illness begins.

1915   *The Voyage Out*; Leonard and Woolf move to Hogarth House.

1917   Woolfs start the Hogarth Press in March.

1919   *Night and Day.*

1922   *Jacob's Room* becomes the first full-length novel published by the Hogarth Press.

1924   The Hogarth Press moves to 52 Tavistock Square.

1925   *Mrs. Dalloway*; love affair with Vita Sackville-West begins.

1927   *To the Lighthouse.*

1928   *Orlando.*

1929   *A Room of One's Own.*

1931   *The Waves.*

1934   Roger Fry dies.

1937   *The Years.*

1939   Hogarth Press moved to 37 Mecklenburgh Square.

1940   *Roger Fry: A Biography*; Hogarth Press moved to Letchworth.

1941   Woolf drowns herself in the River Ouse on March 28; Leonard publishes some of her writings; *Between the Acts* (posthumous).

Works by Virginia Woolf

Novels

The Voyage Out, 1915
Night and Day, 1919
Jacob's Room, 1922
Mrs. Dalloway, 1925
To the Lighthouse, 1927
Orlando: A Biography, 1928
The Waves, 1931
The Years, 1937
Between the Acts, 1941 (ed. Leonard Woolf)

Essays

"Mr. Bennett and Mrs. Brown," 1924
The Common Reader, First Series, 1925
A Room of One's Own, 1929
The Common Reader, Second Series, 1932
"Three Guineas," 1938
"The Death of the Moth" and Other Essays, 1942 (ed. Leonard Woolf)
"The Moment" and Other Essays, 1947 (ed. Leonard Woolf)
"The Captain's Death Bed" and Other Essays, 1950 (ed. Leonard Woolf)
Granite and Rainbow, 1958 (ed. Leonard Woolf)
Contemporary Writers, 1965
Collected Essays (4 vols.), 1966–1967 (ed. Leonard Woolf)

Short Stories

"The Mark on the Wall," 1917 (published in *Two Stories*)
"Kew Gardens," 1919
Monday or Tuesday, 1921
"Flush: A Biography," 1933
"A Haunted House" and Other Short Stories, 1944 (ed. Leonard Woolf)
A Cockney's Farming Experiences, 1973 (early works)
"Mrs. Dalloway's Party," 1973

Nonfiction

Roger Fry: A Biography, 1940

A Writer's Diary, 1953 (ed. Leonard Woolf)

Many collections of Woolf's essays and letters are available, as are selections from her diaries. She wrote her most important autobiographical works, aside from her diaries, at various points in her life; these were later collected and published as *Moments of Being* (ed. Jeanne Schulkind, 1976). Woolf prepared several of these pieces for the Memoir Club, of which numerous Bloomsbury personalities were members.

Bibliography

Bell, Anne Olivier, and Andrew McNeillie. *The Diary of Virginia Woolf* (five volumes). Hogarth Press, 1977–1984.

Bell, Quentin. *Virginia Woolf: A Biography.* Harcourt Brace, 1972 (two volumes).

Leaska, Mitchell. *Granite and Rainbow: The Hidden Life of Virginia Woolf.* Farrar, Straus, & Giroux, 1998.

Lee, Hermione. *Virginia Woolf.* Chatto & Windus, 1996.

Lehmann, John. *Virginia Woolf.* Thames & Hudson, 1999.

Majumdar, Robin, and Aden McLauren, eds. *Virginia Woolf: The Critical Heritage.* Routledge, 1997.

Nicolson, Nigel. *Virginia Woolf.* Viking Penguin, 2000.

———, and Joanne Trautman, eds. *The Letters of Virginia Woolf* (six volumes). Hogarth Press, 1975–1984.

Schulkind, Jeanne, ed. *Moments of Being.* Harvest Books, 1985.

Woolf, Leonard. *Downhill All the Way: An Autobiography of the Years 1919 to 1939.* Harvest Books, 1966.

———, ed. *A Writer's Diary: Being Extracts from the Diary of Virginia Woolf.* Harvest Books, 1973.

Apter, T.E. *Virginia Woolf: A Study of Her Novels.* New York University Press, 1979.

Banks, Joanne Trautman. *Congenial Spirits. The Selected Letters of Woolf.* Hogarth Press, 1989.

Bell, Anne Olivier, and Andrew McNeillie. *The Diary of Virginia Woolf* (five volumes). Hogarth Press, 1977–1984.

Bell, Quentin. *Bloomsbury.* Weidenfeld and Nicolson, 1968.

———. *Bloomsbury Recalled.* Columbia University Press, 1997.

———. *Virginia Woolf: A Biography.* Harcourt Brace, 1972 (two volumes).

———, Virginia Nicholson, and Alen MacWeeney (photographer). *Charleston: A Bloomsbury House and Garden.* Frances Lincoln Ltd., 2002.

Bennett, Joan. *Virginia Woolf: Her Art as a Novelist.* Second edition. Cambridge University Press, 1964.

Briggs, Julia, ed. *Virginia Woolf: Introductions to the Major Works.* Virago Press, 1994.

Clements, Patricia, and Isobel Grundy, eds. *Virginia Woolf: New Critical Essays.* Vision, 1983.

Di Battista, Maria. *Virginia Woolf's Major Novels.* Yale University Press, 1980.

Gordon, Lyndall. *Virginia Woolf: A Writer's Life.* Oxford University Press, 1984.

Homans, Margaret, ed. *Virginia Woolf: A Collection of Critical Essays.* Simon and Schuster Prentice-Hall, 1993.

Hussey, Mark. *Virginia Woolf A to Z: A Comprehensive Reference for Students, Teachers, and Common Readers to her Life, Works, and Critical Reception.* Oxford University Press, 1996.

Jacobus, Mary. "The Difference of View." *Reading Women: Essays in Feminist Criticism.* Methuen, 1986.

Leaska, Mitchell. *Granite and Rainbow: The Hidden Life of Virginia Woolf.* Farrar, Straus, & Giroux, 1998.

Lee, Hermione. *Virginia Woolf.* Chatto & Windus, 1996.

Lehmann, John. *Virginia Woolf.* Thames & Hudson, 1999.

Further Reading

Marcus, Jane. *Virginia Woolf and the Languages of Patriarchy.* Indiana University Press, 1987.

Nicolson, Nigel. *Virginia Woolf.* Viking Penguin, 2000.

Poole, Roger. *The Unknown Virginia Woolf.* Cambridge University Press, 1978.

Reid, Panthea. *Art and Affection: A Life of Virginia Woolf.* Oxford University Press, 1996.

Roe, Sue, and Susan Sellers, eds. *The Cambridge Companion to Virginia Woolf.* Cambridge University Press, 2000.

Rosenberg, Beth Carole, and Jeanne Dubino, eds. *Virginia Woolf and the Essay.* St. Martin's Press, 1997.

Rose, Phyllis. *Woman of Letters: A Life of Virginia Woolf.* Oxford University Press, 1978.

Shone, Richard. *The Art of Bloomsbury.* Princeton University Press, 2000.

Silver, Brenda. *Virginia Woolf Icon.* University of Chicago Press, 1999.

Stape, J.H. *Virginia Woolf: Interviews and Recollections.* Macmillan, 1995.

Strachey, Lytton. *Eminent Victorians.* Harvest Books, 2002.

———. *Queen Victoria.* Harvest Books, 2002.

Todd, Pamela. *Bloomsbury at Home.* Harry N. Abrams, 2000.

Willis, J.H. *Leonard and Virginia Woolf as Publishers.* University Press of Woolf, 1992.

Woolf, Leonard. *Downhill All the Way: An Autobiography of the Years 1919 to 1939.* Harvest Books, 1966.

Wussow, Helen, ed. *New Essays on Virginia Woolf.* Contemporary Research Press, 1995.

Zwerdling, Alex. *Virginia Woolf and the Real World.* University of California Press, 1986.

Web sites

The International Virginia Woolf Society
www.utoronto.ca/IVWS/

The Literature Network: Virginia Woolf
www.online-literature.com/virginia_woolf/

Books of the World: Woolf, Virginia
www.booksfactory.com/writers/woolf.htm

ELiterature: Virginia Woolf
www.eliterature.com.ar/woolf_virginia/

Project Gutenberg of Australia: Virginia Woolf
gutenberg.net.au/pages/woolf.html

Virginia Woolf's Psychiatric History
ourworld.compuserve.com/homepages/malcolmi/vwframe.htm
A true achievement. This site's author, himself an accomplished psychiatrist, thoroughly and insightfully explores Woolf's psychology, her attacks, her literary output, and even her doctors. Well worth a long visit.

Index

Index

Index

Index

and decision to become writer, 23, 31, 33

and diary, 6, 8, 14-15, 28, 39, 50, 56, 70, 72, 79, 95, 102, 108

and experiences in writing, 24, 26, 28, 29, 31-33, 43, 79, 81, 85, 87, 93, 104

and family newspaper, 24, 26

and final novel, 108-110

and first novel, 50-51, 108-110

and first published essays, 16, 31-33

and form, 96

and letters, 14-15, 24, 28, 29, 50, 51, 56

and nonfiction, 43, 88, 90-91, 102, 105, 108

and popularity in America, 12, 14, 17, 33, 100, 104

and stream of consciousness, 78-79, 84-85

and style, 15-16, 17, 19, 32, 44, 46, 57-58, 61, 65, 66, 70, 73, 75, 78-79, 80, 81-85, 90, 95-96, 102-103

and themes, 14, 16, 17, 43, 46, 50, 58, 66, 81-84, 90-91, 95, 103, 104, 105, 108

and time, 81, 84-85, 96

and writing cycle, 85-90

See also specific titles

World War I, 54, 58, 59-60, 68, 75, 101, 107

World War II, 105, 107-108, 110

Years, The, 14, 56, 63, 102-105, 110

Young, Edward Hilton, 46

Credits

page:

13: Cover reprinted courtesy Time, Inc. Cover image: TimeLife Pictures/Getty Images

18: © HultonlArchive, by Getty Images

22: © Hulton-Deutsch Collection/CORBIS

25: Courtesy Library of Congress, LC-USZ62-128601

30: Courtesy Library of Congress, LC-USZ62-118073

35: © HultonlArchive, by Getty Images

41: © HultonlArchive, by Getty Images

45: © Tate Archive, London/Art Resource, NY

49: © Hulton-Deutsch Collection/CORBIS

55: © Michael Boys/CORBIS

62: © HultonlArchive, by Getty Images

65: Courtesy of Cynthia Burgess

71: Courtesy of Cynthia Burgess

74: © Tate Archive, London/Art Resource, NY

77: © HultonlArchive, by Getty Images

89: © E.O. Hoppé/CORBIS

94: © Tate Gallery, London/Art Resource, NY

99: © E.O. Hoppé/CORBIS

106: © Archivo Iconografico, S.A./CORBIS

109: © Archivo Iconografico, S.A./CORBIS

Cover: Associated Press, AP

Contributors

Clifford Mills is a writer and editor living in Meriden, New Hampshire. He has compiled a volume of essays about J.D. Salinger and has written many essays about the environment and medicine. In addition, he has edited books for a wide range of literary genres and for several scientific disciplines at John Wiley and Sons and Oxford University Press. He is an avid collector of Hogarth Press books.

Congresswoman Betty McCollum (Minnesota, Fourth District) is the second woman from Minnesota ever to have been elected to Congress. Since the start of her first term of office in 2000, she has worked diligently to protect the environment and to expand access to health care, and she has been an especially strong supporter of education and women's health care. She holds several prominent positions in the House Democratic Caucus and enjoys the rare distinction of serving on three House committees at once. In 2001, she was appointed to represent the House Democrats on the National Council on the Arts, the advisory board of the National Endowment for the Arts.